TELL-TALES 4

ACKNOWLEDGEMENTS

We would like to thank our writers both past and present... Jacob Ross, James Miller and Tom Lee for taking time out of their schedules to read the manuscript... Peepal Tree Press for their support and guidance... Monique Roffey for her hard work and dedication to this project... Sherin Nicole for giving us such an imaginative, striking cover... And the Arts Council England, namely Charles Beckett, for his continuing support.

Most of all thanks to our readers; hope you enjoy this one!

Courttia Newland, Nii Ayikwei Parkes and Sharmila Chauhan

TELL-TALES 4

EDITED

COURTTIA NEWLAND AND MONIQUE ROFFEY

P E E P A L   T R E E

First published in Great Britain in 2009
Peepal Tree Press Ltd
17 King's Avenue
Leeds LS6 1QS
England

ISBN13: 9781845230791

ARTS COUNCIL
ENGLAND   Peepal Tree gratefully acknowledges Arts Council support

CONTENTS

TELL TALES 4 – INTRODUCTION

MONIQUE ROFFEY

It's no secret that the short story is a much neglected literary form in the UK and has been for some time. Apart from a smattering of competitions and handful of literary magazines, there's very little credible or widely accessible editorial space for today's working writer to publish their short stories. While it's possible, in the US, for a writer to carve out an *entire career* as a short story writer, this isn't possible this side of the Atlantic. The publishing industry doesn't trust the selling power of the short story. Apparently, there's no readership for short stories, not enough people read or enjoy them – there's no mass appeal. Crudely put, short stories don't make money. In 2008, writers would find it easier to sell balls of their hair or small piles of their fingernail clippings than a collection of short stories to a mainstream publisher.

This is hard to understand when Annie Proulx's short story, 'Brokeback Mountain', from the collection of that name, was made into a mainstream award-winning motion picture in 2006. Hard to understand, when, in fact, there are numerous examples of short stories which have earnt authors and publishers pots of money, awards and readers – in the form of the printed word as well as film adaptation: Daphne du Maurier made a few quid with 'The Birds' and 'Don't Look Now', Philip K. Dick with 'Total Recall', Frank Rooney with a story called 'Cyclist's Raid' which became *The Wild One*. 'All About Eve', '2001: a Space Odyssey', 'The Swimmer', by John Cheever, were all short stories which were developed and made into films. All began life as short works of literary merit and critical acclaim – and all have been read, seen and loved by millions all over the planet.

In the light of this baffling conundrum, huge credit goes to writer and literary activist Courttia Newland for establishing the Tell Tales Collective in 2004, an organisation exclusively committed to supporting the short story form. To date, Tell Tales (with the help of Arts Council England) have published four anthologies of short stories and organised three national tours promoting the work of over eighty short story writers based in the UK and abroad. These anthologies have showcased work by established and prize-winning authors and apprentice writers alike; writers new to the literary arena have been published and read their work aloud alongside the likes of Maggie Gee, Matt Thorne and Romesh Gunesekera.

Talking of planets, *Tell Tales Four* has an international theme – The Global Village. Over a period of three months (November 2007–February 2008) we cast our net as widely as possible to make this volume representative of its theme. Our plan was to pull in exemplary short stories from writers all around the world; we hoped to find stories with a broad range of theme and voice and wanted to attract writers with diverse backgrounds of culture and life experience, all which would be reflected in the stories themselves. Age, gender, ethnicity – yes, we wanted the collection to come together as a composite picture of *all* the voices now attempting the short form. And so requests for submissions were sent to writers and MA writing programmes in the UK, USA. Africa and the Caribbean. We advertised on the Tell Tales website, on Facebook and contacted our agents and friends. Our efforts were immediately rewarded and we received over 150 submissions, many by well established literary authors. After months of reading and hours of heated editorial debate, we feel the 26 stories published in this collection represent the cream of the submissions we received and enough talent to send publishers, agents and Hollywood producers into a frenzy.

This collection is dark. Dark and funny. Sixteen of the

writers are women, ten are men. Ten of the writers are well established authors, the list being headed by a literary super-star from the Caribbean, Olive Senior. The rest are writers of great promise, mostly on an MA, who are taking their first steps into fiction. The stories are set in the UK, USA, Africa, India, Switzerland, cyberspace, a call centre, the future. Three are set in the Caribbean, reflecting my own literary tastes and background. Most are ambitious. There's no pussy-footing around the margins of life's human experience, no 'small' stories in this collection; all these writers tackle the grand themes of love, sex and death and war, also political corruption, immigration, even, yes, global warming. Some like Drew Gummerson's 'Gus', or Sophie Woolley's 'Elusive Arthur', make the reader laugh out loud. Some, such as Kay Sexton's 'The Economy of Violence' make us shudder and pause for thought. One or two, such as Ginny Bailey's 'The Sand Eaters' make us want to cry.

The stories themselves, in terms of content, deal with conflict, crime and politics and are sometimes brutal. There's ritual murder, the death of a drug-dealer by cycle chain and acid, a woman who stabs her boss and enforced lover, a man, already dead, who finds out he's dead, a driver for an aid agency who kills a would-be hijacker. In all, I counted seven deaths (mostly grisly murders), four drug-related stories, two ghost-related stories, one tale of the aftermath of genocide, one tale of the aftermath of the war in Yugoslavia. But there's lots of love too, some sex, a game of scrabble, a talking dog robot and wasps appearing in October.

Courttia and I agreed on all these stories jointly; there's not one we felt didn't belong or was off-theme. As writers our-selves, we had to examine our own tastes as to why we both enjoyed such predominantly grim stories. Maybe because each has been told with such skill and care that they read as *important* rather than sordid or titillating or weird. Together, these stories form the composite picture-of-our-times we were looking for: a zeitgeist collection which reflects the ideas and concerns of writers all over the world capturing impressions of human life and writing in the short story form.

Tell Tales Four is also a collection about *place*. Many of the stories give the reader brief but sharply focused glimpses into life and culture of other countries. The stories are set against vividly detailed towns, rivers, villages, neighbourhoods and landscapes. They are evocative and particular: we experience harmony, chaos and human death-life rituals along the banks of the River Ganges in Nina Joshi's 'Through her Eyes'. In Keith Jardim's 'Caribbean Honeymoon' we see bronze statues of politicians with indifferent gazes, feel the dead-salt air of an unnamed port that could be any port in the Antilles, see the smoke of bush fires floating in the sky above the city like an amber necklace. In 'Cycle Chain Acid', by Rahul Mitra, we meet the pimps, whores, dope-dealers and rickshaw-pullers of Hyderabad. We visit the banks of the cold, eerie Thames, a hotel in Dubai; join an aid convoy in Africa. We get to feel that these authors are experts in their topographical terrain as well as story subject matter; they know these places intimately, and give us perfect, thin slices of life from these other places.

This collection is dark, funny and predominantly *female*. Mostly written by women, there isn't one story set in once-conventional female territory, (the home, marriage, the trials of childcare and domesticity). Most of the women writing here not only write about life out in the world, but also take technical risks with narrative devices. Frances Merivale, with 'In Transit', gives us a humane and touching story about a sexually predatory woman. Julia H. King, in 'Teamwork Response Action Performance' portrays the harsh realities and sterility of working in a multi-national call-centre. Foluke Taylor, in 'Power Trip', writes from the POV of a man on holiday in Africa who gets his come-uppance. Olive Senior writes for the POV of a child who witnesses his father's murder. Catherine Smith writes her sad story about Alzheimer's mostly in emails. Sophie Woolley writes about the future. Patsy Antoine's macabre story of ritual murder, 'The Last Rites of an English Rose', is told backwards. There's more here than the linear and conventional *as-if-real* story. We see enormous range in terms of content and great versatility of style.

It was a great honour to edit this anthology. A great pleasure too. More than anything, it has been an affirmation that the short story form is alive and well. These twenty-six writers have turned in perfect examples of the form. These stories make the collection hard to put down. Enjoy!

Monique Roffey
London
May 2008

www.moniqueroffey.co.uk

SILENT

OLIVE SENIOR

What endured in him was not the remembrance of noise. Not the shots ricocheting in the small room, not the sound of tearing and splintering, not the aftershocks. What remained was the sudden silence that sucked him in and shut the noise out. Only the day before, his teacher had described the eye of the hurricane, that calm, silent centre in the middle of the storm. That sudden stillness before whoosh, from the other direction, the second, more terrifying wind came bursting through. In the heart of this hurricane, he listened for the terror returning, but heard nothing. Not the crack of the door kicked in again, not his father jumping up and reaching for his gun and falling in the very action, not the blasts, the ripping sounds. He thought, in a wondering kind of way: so this is what it feels like to be deaf, and inside this new space, he found himself surprised and glad to learn something new, something he could hold on to.

Under the bed where his mother thrust all three of them, his little brother and sister clutch him so tightly they are like warm glue melting against his back. They do not let go even when he begins to crawl to where he can look and see what is happening. Through the space where the pink chenille bedspread ends a foot from the rough plank floor, he will watch, mesmerised, the blood pumping out of his father and creeping ever so slowly towards him. He will watch the sneakers of the two men dancing around as they toss the place as if searching for something, watch as one comes close and lifts a corner of the mattress, bends down to look underneath and sees the bundle of children, his face framed by the metal bedspring in bars of cruel light. In that sudden glare, Joel knows he should close his eyes but he cannot; he knows the men anyway, they are part of his father's posse. After a suffocating moment the man drops the mattress and when nothing else happens, Joel can't stop himself, he has to crawl out further to see more of the room, to see his mother.

He sees, first, her toes tightly clenched in her slippers, then as he pushes his head further out, her hands rigid at her sides. Pulled by the tension of her body, his eyes travel up past her arms, and he sees the gun at her head, her mouth opening and closing. He quickly retreats then, closes his eyes tightly and waits for that final shot. But no sound comes.

He has no idea how long he lay there clutching Clive and Jessamine; it could have been days or weeks or years, till he senses someone crawling under the bed, feels his mother's trembling as she locks her body on to them tightly, wordlessly.

After a time, his mother's grip loosens. She raises her body and half turns to face the door as he turns towards her, his chest heavy inside him. She puts her finger to her lips and gives him a look that means 'Stay here' and gets out from under the bed just as the door bursts in again. Police, he can tell from their boots even before they call out. His little brother and sister stay silent, not even a whimper though he can smell them for they have soiled themselves, him too. But he knows he needs to be quiet for police are dangerous bad men, everyone knows.

He watches as they lower their M16s to poke at the body on the floor which the flies and ants have already colonized in the rising heat, wipe the congealed blood off their boots on the small rug Miss Simms, his mother's employer, had given her at Christmas and which no one in the family is allowed to even touch much less walk on. And though he still can't hear, all his other senses are heightened, sickness rising in him from all the smells, nasty smells from sweaty bodies, dried blood, bodily waste. As if all the everyday noxious odours of the yard and lane, the entire neighbourhood, the world, are rising up to stifle the air in the room.

He sees the others arrive, the plainclothes men, and the first one leaning down to get a good look at the man on the floor smiling broadly. Others come in to stare at the body, smile and give each other high fives, strut around and kick with their sneakers and heavy boots at the furniture and possessions strewn on the floor. He can see his mother shaking her head up and down, opening her mouth, turning and moving her body, gesturing with her hands, moving her feet. Then they take her outside.

He closes his eyes again and drifts back onto the silent island on which they are marooned under the bed, he and his little brother and sister who are now wide awake but silent too, both with their thumbs in their mouths and still glued so tightly to him he feels as if they will never again be separated from one another. It is as if they are sealed off, hearing nothing of the clamour outside. Nothing from the tenement yard, from the laneway full of curious people, nothing of the everyday sounds, the screams or shouts or curses, the raucous laughter, the music blasting from every doorway, the motorbikes and cars revving up and down the narrow streets and lanes, the scatter of gunshots that near and far pattern night and day like the barking of the mangy dogs.

Then everything happens at once; his mother pulling them out from under the bed, lifting up the baby and leading them outside through the silently staring crowd to the bathroom where she washes them off, herself too, while he watches the water run red into the hole in the concrete. She rubs them dry and puts them in clean clothes and a policewoman is helping her to dress Jess and Clive and next thing the policewoman is taking Jess and the bag with Jess's things and he and Clive are being pushed into the back of a police car.

"Mama," he tries to speak but nothing comes out. She leans inside the car window and puts her hand on his head in that gentle way he loves. "Is alright Jo-Jo. I come to the station and get you later. Look after your brother and sister for me. You are the man in charge." Thinking about it much later, he decides he must have been lip reading for the only thing he actually hears is: 'the man in charge'.

15

He opens his mouth to speak but again nothing comes, as if the bullets were like a hand passing across his mouth to seal it. As the policeman shuts the car door and they drive off, his last view is of his mother standing there surrounded by armed policemen and TV cameras and the street full of curious people. A scene so ordinary and everyday in his neighbourhood he would usually just push his way through such a crowd on his way to school, even if the bodies were there in full view, not even bothering to look or stop and find out who the latest victim was, the whys or the wherefores. He just took it to be the way life was lived. He would hear the details at school anyway, the children were always so full of it, playing out the death scene like the actors in some gangster movie – Pi! Pi! Pi! At the sound of gunshots, real or imagined, they all threw themselves flat and pressed their bodies to the ground. Now in the back of the police car, Joel already feels so far away from the scene, from himself, it is as if none of it existed.

He rouses himself when they come to the police station and he fully expects them to be locked up in a cell. But in the reception area they put him and Clive to sit on a wooden bench against a far wall and the policewoman who has taken Jess inside brings her back sucking on a bottle and hands her over to him saying something and smiling.

But just at that moment pandemonium breaks out at the station with armed police in riot gear rushing in and out, and from their movements he can tell that radios and walkie-talkies are crackling, the station phones are ringing, voices are raised, orders barked. All the adults seem in such a frenzy that the children on the wooden bench press themselves against the wall, for safety, and are soon forgotten. After a while Joel moves Jess off his lap and puts her to sit on the seat beside him so Clive who is nodding off can lie on the bench and put his head in his lap. Jess doesn't protest as she normally would, she leans against Joel and he puts his arm around her, wondering if she and Clive have also fallen deaf and dumb.

Joel is dying of thirst, and his jeans and t-shirt are soaked from the heat of the day rising and the clammy bodies of his brother and sister. His feet inside his sneakers suddenly feel slick and damp and uncomfortable for he isn't wearing socks. He contorts his body so as not to disturb the little ones and lifts up first one foot and then the other to take the shoes off, glad he hadn't done up the laces. They are the same make as the sneakers worn by the men the night before, by the plainclothes detectives, the favoured footwear of all real men, like his father. He'd brought them all new shoes from his last trip to New York which meant crossing off another thing from his long list of promises, like moving them out of the tenement and into a real house, soon.

Joel remembers how proud he was to wear his new sneakers to school, at the same time worried that someone would beat him up to steal them; now they feel like fire consuming his feet. He pulls them off and drops them on the floor, then he kicks them hard under the bench and wriggles his toes. He is dying to lie on the bench and go to sleep himself. But he knows he can't. He has to stay alert. He is the man in charge.

It is much later when things have quietened down at the station that someone notices them. Joel sees the policemen and woman looking at them and talking and he wonders where they will take them and if they will shoot them and why his mother hasn't come. He knows she will come, for she has never let him down yet. But when? And if the policemen take them somewhere, how will she find them?

Just then the policewoman comes over and she takes them in turn to the washroom and makes them use the toilet and wash their hands and faces, talking to them all the while though he can't make out what she is saying. A policeman takes Jess's bottle and Joel is surprised when he brings it back that he doesn't wait on the policewoman but he himself takes the baby in his arms to feed her and parades with her around, other police teasing him and laughing. Another policeman comes in with bags from Kentucky Fried. Joel didn't know he was hungry till he catches the smell of chicken and fries and he is pleasantly surprised when the policeman hands a bag each to him and Clive. He didn't know he could get through a large Pepsi so fast.

After this, Clive falls asleep again but Joel stays alert, watching out for Jess whom the police have taken away into another room. By the time they bring her back, in clean nappies and clutching another full bottle, he can tell that it is late in the day for they have switched on the lights and the little bit of sky he can see outside is darkening. His mother hasn't come and the big policeman in charge is looking at them in a vexed way, and talking to the policewoman. He knows they are going to move them somewhere or even take them back home. But what if his mother isn't there? And the gunmen come back? He is sure they took his father's guns, so he won't even have a weapon to defend them, little Clive and Jessamine.

Then his mother does come in the door, in a rush, followed by a well dressed lady whom he knows as Miss Simms, one of the women she does days work for. Miss Simms is young and pretty and rich for she is always sending them presents. His mother and Miss Simms both turn and smile at them but when he makes to move, his mother signals for him to stay where he is. He can see them talking to the police and next thing the police are rushing them all through the back entrance and into Miss Simms' car which is parked there and she is driving away in a tearing hurry and not in the direction of home either. His mother and Miss Simms never say a word until they are well out of their part of town that people like Miss Simms never visit.

On the back seat the three of them are sitting down low as their mother instructed them, so they can't be seen, and she herself is crouched down in the front seat so it looks like Miss Simms is the only one in the car. They travel for a good long time like this before their mother sits up and Joel passes Jess over to her.

After that it is as if Miss Simms with her long wavy hair and thin brown hands on the wheel cannot stop driving, as if she is the one that has to carry on, carry them far away from danger that stalks them, through streets Joel has never seen, past gardens and trees and houses as big as churches, way past where Miss Simms herself lives, for he has been there. They are climbing higher and higher towards the mountains he can see in the distance till finally they leave the city far behind. Through the open windows he can feel a fresh breeze blowing, air that is cleaner than anything he has felt in his life. All around the land is dark, except for the light now and then of a house in the distance, the occasional car headlights suddenly lancing the night, approaching like monsters, then abandoning them to the dark. He has never seen such darkness before, yet he isn't afraid. He is kneeling on the back seat so he can look out the rear window and wriggle his bare toes. From this vantage point, he can monitor the splendour of the dark hills that are closing ranks behind them like guards. Witness to the purity of the clear skies above and the embedded stars, that are shimmering and pulsing, like gunshots. But far, far away. And silent.

GRACE'S LOVE THEME

MICHAEL A. GONZALES

Two days after Christmas break in 1978, Grace Campbell joined our 8th grade class at St. Catherine's of Genoa in Harlem. Dressed in a crisp Catholic girl skirt and white blouse, she stood in front of the dusty blackboard, fidgeting under the white fluorescent lights while being introduced by the teacher.

Overhead, there was a row of portraits of famous poets including Langston Hughes and Edgar Allen Poe. Sister Marquez said, "Our newest student, Grace Campbell, has moved here with her family from the island of Jamaica." With her soft voice, she had a way of making the mundane sound magical. "Please make her feel welcome."

Listening to the nun's introduction, I stared at Grace's lovely face. She was the colour of peanut butter. Her freshly pressed hair reminded one of the luxurious tresses in shampoo commercials. Her radiant eyes, with their full lashes, revealed a fusion of fear and wonder.

"Pleased to meet you," she said, shyly. A shapely girl, her accent was thick as honey and just as sweet. A few kids laughed at her voice, but I was pleased because Sister Marquez assigned her a desk next to mine.

For the remainder of the day we tried to avoid each other's curious glances.

"That little new chick sure is fine," blurted my best friend Smokey as we walked to his grandmother's house during lunchtime. It had snowed a few days before, and the slippery ground was covered with slush. "She play her cards right, homegirl can get it," he continued, swirling his bony pelvis. At fourteen, our hormones were already out of control.

Every couple days or so we walked the few blocks to the old lady's crib instead of suffering through the slop in the school cafeteria. In the winter months, she heated-up heaping bowls of beef stew with pieces of potatoes or hearty portions of homemade soup filled with chunks of chicken.

Although it was freezing outside, it was Smokey's words that made me shiver. Our identical black wool hats were pulled down below our ears. All of a sudden I developed a serious attitude.

"What difference does it make to you, Smokey?" I screamed. "Jesus, don't you have enough girlfriends."

I spat a glob of mucus onto the icy ground. Smokey simply stared at me, and smiled.

"Ahhh, give it a rest," said Smokey. Looking directly in my eyes, he tried to stare me down. "You know jealousy is a very ugly emotion. It's one of the seven deadly sins for a reason. Anyway, I ain't plotting on that island girl, man." Seconds before the traffic light changed, the chubby crossing guard blew a silver whistle. For a few minutes, we seemed to be frozen in time. "Besides," said Smokey, breaking the spell, "I don't much care for coconuts."

A yellow school bus crowded with retarded children crept down Broadway. The unruly kids rocked back and forth in their seats. A few smashed their soft skulls on the dirty windows while others drooled down the front of already stained shirts.

"What do you mean by 'coconuts'?" I asked. The traffic screeched to a stop, and the bus slid a few feet. A few of the big headed kids screamed frantically from behind the thick glass.

"That's what my father calls West Indians," he laughed as we approached the decaying front of his grandmother's massive apartment building. Countless television antennas lined the rooftop like a metal forest. "He says they ain't nothing but coconuts."

"Well, I happen to like coconuts," I said, thinking of the tropical ices I bought from the pizza joint on sweltering summer days. The streets were swarming with loud folks taking advantage of the weather: children screamed, mush-mouthed drunks talked junk and cars blew exhaust fumes in our faces. Since our hood was such a gumbo of various folks, from old-school Jews to "speaka no english" Dominicans, homeboy's prejudice surprised me.

Smokey pushed open the busted building door. The chipped marble hallway had seen better days. The trash behind the staircase smelled of spoiled milk and old diapers. After boarding the tiny deathtrap, the elevator crawled to the fourth floor. With its scarred walls, the tight steel box smelled of fresh piss. "Don't worry, nigga. Grace ain't my cup of tea no way. It's not like your scared ass knows what to do, but feel free to make that move."

"Glad I got your permission," I snapped as the elevator door slid open.

Perhaps the worse part about having old friends was the fact that they knew too much about you. Smokey was right. Often my inability to speak in complete sentences to the opposite sex was worse than those retarded children on the bus. As we stepped into the dimly lit hallway I was determined to make a change.

The spicy smell of spaghetti sauce simmering on a hot stove filled the dingy corridor. The melodramatic chatter of a soap opera diva drifted from the black and white TV set behind the rickety door; with cold hands, Smokey knocked hard.

A minute passed before we heard pink slippers sliding across the foyer floor. Smokey's granny welcomed us with wrinkled arms.

Winter dragged into spring, and as the months slowly passed, Grace and I became friends. In the school we shared #2 pencils and talked about Motown singles, television shows and home-work assignments. We shared a passion for words, and often exchanged books.

After my homeboys learnt that Grace was the second cousin of Grandmaster Dynamite, a local hip-hop DJ who spun at neighbourhood block parties and a local hang-out called Da

Bassment, even they began to accept her into our clique. Yet, after three months in the city of skyscrapers and strive, Grace was still a stranger in a strange land.

"I'll be honest with you," she confessed one afternoon. It was an unseasonably warm day, and we had stopped at Poppi's Pizza to get an Italian ice; of course, I ordered coconut. "This is not the America I had anticipated."

One of the midget gypsy fortune-tellers from the store next door stood next to her puffing on a thick stogie.

"I don't understand what you mean," I answered. Sometimes her logic puzzled me.

"I mean, when I was back home I would watch American television shows. I saw shows like *Andy Griffith* and *Leave It to Beaver,* and I thought the States was full of pretty lawns and picket fences. But, not this."

"It's not so bad," I said, as we continued on to her apartment house on 147th Street and Amsterdam. "I'm sure you'll get used to it here. You just got to give it time."

There was sadness in her eyes. "That's just it, Dorian," Grace sighed. "I'm thinking about going home at the end of the school year. My grandmother has been ill since the family came to New York and I want to go be with her. Maybe I'll come back, but right now she needs me."

A week before Easter, Sister Marquez assigned the class to write poems about whatever they felt. Grace's bittersweet composition was stunning. Tilting her head as she read, it seemed as though a billowing breeze blew lyrical words into her ears and over her delicate tongue.

She had composed a strange, yet beautiful poem called "Yardie Girl" about her native Trench Town parish of Mojo Pen: of boys with machetes serving sweet coconut milk from the green shell and old men playing dominos down the road; of old goats whining and young babies crying and the ocean splashing in the distance; of early morning cocks that crowed in the middle of dusty roads while an old man prepared ackee for breakfast; of wrinkled old women reading *The Gleaner* while jerk chicken stewed in a rustic metal cooker; of the

Rastas who sang dreadlock guitar blues in the afternoon shadows and danced in the moonlight while Saturday night sound-systems blasted music from massive speakers.

Grace's words made me all warm inside. Her poem had transported me to her place in the sun. Listening to her heartfelt verses, a feeling of passion surged through my blood like a million shooting stars screaming across the sky.

"Man, that bullshit didn't even rhyme," mumbled Smokey. "What kind of poem don't even rhyme?"

Still, it was after hearing her poetry that I finally got the balls to ask Grace if she wanted to go to the movies on Easter Sunday.

"It'll be fun," I said. That April afternoon the sun was shining bright, but it was still chilly. Grace looked at me and giggled. My first instinct was to flee down the hill and act like no words had ever been exchanged. It seemed so much easier to simply return to stickball games or skelly tournaments or leaping across rooftops with Smokey. "What's so funny?" I asked, scared and indignant.

"Nothing, really," she said. "It's just for the past few months, you've been really nice and everything. Almost like a brother. I just didn't realize you liked me like that."

I decided not to mention that if it wasn't for my crew's constant badgering, specifically Smoke's veiled threats to "develop a taste for coconuts", that I might have never asked.

"Yeah," I said. "But this should be fun. It'll be a bunch of us, but still it should be fun." Grace grinned and nodded her head.

For the next seven days, nothing could shatter my beaming smile.

It wasn't until I watched the weekly marquee changers that I realized the Easter Sunday double feature was to be *Sparkle* & *Super Fly*. The fact that both flicks had sweet soundtracks composed by Curtis Mayfield was merely another reason to rejoice.

Come Easter morning the sun was the brightest it had been in months; it was a pleasant spring day of mellow warmth and laughter. I had just finished my eleven o'clock altar-boy duties, and was trying to make it to *The Tapia* within the hour.

"Hurry up, ya slow..." I yelled at Smokey. Sweating like slaves, we rushed the six blocks to the theatre where Grace and the rest of the crew was already waiting.

A vision of island girl splendour, Grace looked like a secret garden of floral delights. She had on a stunning peasant blouse with tiny artificial red roses dripping down the sleeves, a crocheted below-the-knee skirt that emphasized her buxom bottom and white boots embroidered with handmade golden butterflies and delicate daisies; around her waist was a beige leather belt decorated with coral and turquoise on the buckle – to match her turquoise-painted manicured fingernails. She wore dainty earrings and a silver crucifix around her neck. Her hair looked softer than black velvet.

I realized I had never seen Grace without her school uniform. Who would have known that she would look like a Jamaican Chaka Khan? Between the heat and Grace, I don't know which made me perspire more.

"You look beautiful," I stuttered. "I mean... like, wow." A moment passed before I finally turned and acknowledged my homeboy Voodoo's girlfriend Rhonda, as well as C.C., Smokey and their dates. C.C. was hugged-up with a chick named Maria who was also a student at St. Catherine's while Smokey was palming the neighbourhood fast ass, a girl named Shelia.

"You look quite handsome yourself," said Grace, her piano fingers straightening the tie I was forced to wear with the navy-blue Barney's three-piece suit. While my vines might not have been slick badass street, they were still blaxploitation cool.

"Yeah, a handsome waiter," goofed Voodoo, slapping fives with Smokey and C.C. The three of them wore clothes straight out of the window of A.J. Lester's: maroon double-knits with matching British Walkers and plaid applejack hats. They looked like the murderous Soul Train triplets, but I didn't think of that joke until many days later; Grace's fineness had put a mojo on my mind.

Although I had already seen both films, with Grace by my side everything in the world felt brand new.

"Man, cut the shit and let's get inside before all the good

seats are gone," said Smokey. He held open the glass door until everyone was inside. He tapped me on the shoulder and whispered. "Not bad, nigga. Not bad." He smiled his approval.

"Thanks, duke," I mumbled.

"Just don't die a virgin," he quipped, and winked his eye.

Unlike the usual crowd of street toughs and reefer puffers, the audience looked like a players congregation of baroque brothers and flashy females. There were more gators and snakeskins in the movie house than in the swamplands of the rain forest. *The Tapia* had been transformed into a pimpadelic after-hours spot. Brothers sported the hustler chic of multi-coloured threads and chrome-plated shades, broad brimmed hats and silk shirts.

Opening with a raven's eye view of two junkies in search of a fix on 125th Street, the spooky electric of Curtis Mayfield's "Little Child Running Wild" erupted from the speakers as *Super Fly* was projected on the screen. "Yo, check out Dorian's pops trying to score," howled Voodoo. The entire audience of coifed players laughed rowdily.

"He must be trying to find a hit for your mama," I replied, which sent another hot shot of laughter through the crowd. A few minutes later, when the iceberg cool star Ron O'Neal playing Priest boogalooed onto the screen, a permed-hair motherfucker looking all light-skin and mean (he was laid next to a blonde freak while shovelling white lady up his nose), brothers leapt from their seats as though this was yet another second coming.

In my hour of sexual confusion, the infamous bathtub love scene flashed on the screen. Grace's bare leg rubbed against mine. "What would Priest do in this situation?" I wondered, as a sonic surge of electric ecstasy ignited skyrockets in flight. All I wanted was to caress those slightly hairy legs, taste her buttered popcorn-flavoured tongue and inhale the rose-scented toilet water sprinkled behind her ears. In that special way that is prevalent in women and cats, Grace sensed my fear.

"You're going have to relax," she whispered, spraying rain-drops of saliva that baptized me in her enchanting eroticism. As the king of falsetto soul swooned from the soundtrack ("...*give me your love*," Brother Mayfield crooned), Grace placed her soft hand in my mine. "Don't worry, I'm not going to bite."

As the lovesexy orchestration cascaded over me and Grace, our fingers were tightly entwined. Before I was aware of what had happened, her luscious lips become one with mine.

Everything was nice, everything was slow; it was as though time had stopped and nothing existed in the world except the rapture and riddims of that moment.

WASPS IN OCTOBER

CATHERINE SELBY

Sunlight comes off concrete in rivers. Splashing all the way down the road. The late morning sun makes the double yellow lines flow away and disappear down the drains. Light floods the ground in asphalt blue and waves form in the pits and bumps in the road. Cars travel slowly down here. Windscreens blinking over speed bumps as they try to keep their suspension. It's a match day at home and everyone's after a free parking space.

The houses on the other side of my street have gardens and drives but on this side of the road they are just normal. This side of the road has got a chip shop. It's Saturday dinner time and you can smell they've put new oil in the fryers. You can smell it ten houses down.

A man's hoovering his car on his driveway. He's keeping an eye on the kids riding their bikes in between the slow traffic. Waiting for them to get too close to his house so he can tell them to go.

Next door's kids are playing Three-and-In against my kitchen wall. Mine are round someone else's making costumes for when they go out trick-or-treating later. My house is on the corner. It's a south facing house so it's a sun trap. I've got some time to myself so I've got a deck chair set up half over the front door step and half on the street. Turned-up jean legs and I'm sat back just watching and chatting with my boyfriend.

I've been going out with Jason now for about two and a half years but we don't live together. His ex-wife was crazy and took him for everything when she left him. He says he finds it hard to trust women now. She still turns up at his flat sometimes. Jason says she's why he's got less hair now. He's still quite good looking though. He shaves it all off so some people think he's hard but he's not really.

It's nice to get some time to ourselves though. Jason's got a new stereo in his car that he's messing about with so he's parked up on the kerb sat in the driver's seat with the door open and his legs out. He's listening to the football on the radio. A song comes through next door's front-room window and I sing along. I think I've got a nice voice. He says can you shut up.

It's funny weather. We've not had a proper summer and now it should be autumn but it's not getting any colder. This time last year, well, in a weeks' time – I remember because it's his birthday on the fifth – we had hail. I remember because it brought the guttering down and let water in through that rotting window frame.

Jason fiddles with the tuning on the radio cos he hasn't got it properly. An ice cream van plays the tune off the old Cornetto advert somewhere, the next street back.

"Maybe we're having an Indian summer," I say to him. "It'll make for a wet Christmas. We didn't get much of a summer did we?"

A kid rides past on a broom stick. Face all painted orange with a wicked smile on it. There's a big party three doors down that half the street's going to later. I can't be bothered. I'd rather have a quiet one with Jason. I ask Jason if I have a nice voice. He says Burnley have gone one nil up. I sing, "Just one Cornetto. Give it to me. Delicious ice cream. From Italy."

That ice cream van will come round in the middle of winter if there are kids out. You can be sat having your tea in front of *Coronation Street* and it sings to you like a doorbell. It goes, "Oranges and lemons say the bells of St Clements."

He rolls a cigarette and asks if I can get him a beer. He turns the radio up slightly by pretending it's still not tuned in properly. He doesn't say anything for a while. Checks his stubble in the rear view mirror so he can watch two girls who are about sixteen walk down the road in strappy tops. They haven't had the chance to get fat yet. I say, "The oranges at work aren't as juicy as normal."

I work part-time in a cafe for my friend Marie when the kids are at school. It's a sandwich shop really but it's got some tables and chairs and it's right near the tax office so she does alright at dinner time. She's got one of those juicers to make orange juice with. She charges a fortune because she has to rent the machine – it costs that much to buy – but she reckons people pay more when they think it's healthy. Someone misses a goal and Jason hits the dashboard.

"He's lovely the man that comes and delivers the oranges at Marie's. He brought blood red ones the other day but everyone complained. I loved them. Dark red inside with an orange crust like jam doughnuts. They made a pink orange juice but a few customers thought they were off so we asked to swap back. They've been having problems with the oranges."

Someone's just come back with a goal in the eighty-ninth minute. He thinks the bakers round the corner might be still open if I want to go and get a couple of doughnuts.

"She gets a glass out of four oranges but at the moment you have to put six in the machine to get a full measure. She's told the orange man because he charges her for how many she uses. Nothing he can do, he says. There's a worldwide shortage of oranges. The orange man says all the suppliers went to South Africa for them but they've got none left so they're coming from Brazil which is why they're half as juicy for twice the price. Apparently he was telling her they've had a wet summer down there this year and half the orange crops were wiped out. Even on the continent they're not having proper summers."

There's three minutes of injury time left. "It was on telly that half the country will be under water in a few years if this weather carries on. If it keeps getting hotter in the wrong parts. We'll be stood in three foot of water in our own living rooms next. It'll start with the drains. It was on the news."

This road will be a river. Dark water will come from the ground. Rising and bubbling from the drains. The lines on the road will lie like streaks of oil then the puddles will all muddle together and flow down in any direction you like. Getting in the pits and dips in the road they said they'd fix. Cars will cut their way down the road like they're going through butter left out of the fridge. Until they stop altogether and lie parked in water. Muddy and stuck with rusting.

Dead ponds and lakes will wash up filthy tides of grease in grey rainbows. Waves of stagnant water lapping up the paved drives and making twisted water features of the gardens. It will smell. All the time.

People's belongings that they couldn't tie down or move higher will float by. Eventually the people themselves in rubber boats. Them that live across the road will be the first ones to go.

Kids will sit in trees. The footballs they used to play with bobbing past them on the tide. Bikes given up on. They'll walk to each other's houses on planks. There will be no heat from the houses any more. No clean water. There'll be sandbags on the front door step. Water will come in through the front room windows. Even where it won't reach, nothing will be dry because the water will be in the air, all the time. Everywhere.

Jason switches the radio off cos he'd rather not have it on at all if he's not allowed to listen to it properly. The football's finished and he's missed the last two minutes. He lights the cigarette he rolled before. He aims the smoke out of his car and it stays in the still warm air for a second like a cloud in between his car and my house.

He says he does his bit with the recycling boxes the council bring round every other Wednesday instead of the bins. Although he did see a wasp trying to get out the bathroom window the other day, he says, and you'd think they'd all be dead by the end of October.

The ice cream van comes round again, this time louder and closer and I think about going to get a Cornetto.

THINGS TOO FAR AWAY

JUSTIN HILL

Meili was in the kitchen when Ma Jun came home. "You're back," she called after him as she stared at the slab of meat in front of her. He did not answer and she stood at the chopping board, not knowing where to begin.

"So," she called out, "I killed Project Manager Mu this morning."

There was no answer.

"Did you hear me?"

"Yes," he shouted back, but his voice was distant and unfriendly and uninterested. Meili lifted the muscle, still filmed with milky fat, turned it over so that the thin white tendon lay along the right hand side. She pushed the hair from her face and felt the weight of the cleaver in her hand; didn't know why he was pretending not to believe her.

"So?" she called after a long silence.

"So what?"

"So have you nothing to say?"

"No," Ma Jun called back.

"Then fuck you!" Meili said and slammed the cleaver into the wooden chopping block so hard she couldn't pull it out. She swore and threw the whole lump of meat into the bin. Slammed the door as well. Opened and slammed it again and the third time she slammed it so hard that sharp flakes of paint fell off the wall and sprinkled the concrete floor. Their sudden fall made her think of a Beijing morning long ago when she went outside to catch snowflakes on her tongue, and she grinned and slammed the door again, just as powerfully, but with a smile on her face.

"Where's dinner?" Ma Jun asked an hour or so later.

Meili was smoking Guo Bao cigarettes like a film star. "Fuck off," she said.

Ma Jun helped himself to one of the fags. He stood there, looking at her. She rolled her eyes and pulled out a wad of hundred yuan notes and tossed them towards him.

He counted them while she looked away.

Meili's legs were drawn up to her chin. She had an odd look in her eyes: distant and dreaming, as if she was wondering how she had arrived here, at this moment in the modern world, in the position she was in – why she couldn't have been born a nameless daughter of a Mongolian herdsman, with horses and miles around her, and the freedom to ride all day. Or the pretty daughter of a Beijing professor, with a bedroom to herself, fluffy toys and overprotective parents, a diligent and rich official for a husband. Not a Beijing peasant in a Naxi theme park.

"So did you really kill him?" Ma Jun said.

She looked up and nodded.

"How?" he said.

"I stabbed him," Meili said and pulled out another cigarette.

"Did you fuck him?"

"Yes," she said and stubbed the cigarette out. "I'm hungry."

"Haven't you been to the market?"

"Yes," she said, "but I didn't want to cook."

Her eyes had lost that look. They searched the room and seemed suddenly bored with everything round her. The remote control lay at her side. *Beijing Opera* was on one channel, stock reports on the next, and the last channel had some repeat of last season's *Pop Idol*. They watched till they could no longer think or feel. Only the growing nag of hunger disturbed them.

"I need to eat," he said after an interminable length of time.

She did not turn from the screen. "Get the meat."

"Where is it?"

"In the bin. Get it out and wash it."

Ma Jun washed the pork and Meili remembered what her grandmother had said on the day she left her village in the north. Its name was Walnut Grove Village. Her family had lived there for as long as they could remember, and the people had long memories. Her father had got sick and died when Meili was little, and her mother went to Shanghai to work in a factory and never came back. When she was fifteen, Meili's grandmother had taken her aside. She was old and toothless and poor, too poor to care for a young girl like Meili. Go and find work, her grandmother had told her. I will stay and look after you, Meili had argued, like the characters in old stories, but her grandmother was insistent. You must never come back here, she had said, though I will miss you. Meili had never gone back. Well she had once, but her village had been demolished and there was a golf course now, with hills where there were never hills and holes where her memories had been.

"He cried," she said.

"Who?"

"Project Manager Mu," she said as if he was stupid. "He begged me not to kill him. Said he would give me his bank card. Gave me his password as well. So then I *had* to kill him."

She laughed. Ma Jun nodded. "So how much did you get out?"

"Ten thousand yuan," she said. "It's under the mattress."

Ma Jun lifted up the mattress and whistled between his teeth. The money was so clean it didn't look real.

"Come here," he said. She didn't come so he took her arm and pulled her towards the bed, as Project Manager Mu had done, and threw back the bedspread embroidered with love-birds. Ma Jun moved on top of her, but it was gravity that held Meili down on the bed of hundred yuan notes. On top of Mao's face to be precise, or, it occurred to Meili as she stroked his back, *in* Mao's face.

Afterwards he looked into her eyes, but he might as well have been staring down a well.

"So. Did you really kill him?" he asked.

She nodded. He didn't know why, but he began to believe

34

she really had killed Project Manager Mu. He avoided eye contact with her and looked down at the floor. The woman next door was screaming into the phone: *I can't hear you.* Ma Jun stood up and took a few steps across the room away from her. Meili turned up the television so she couldn't hear the woman next door any more, but something got through and she felt a tear well up and she brought her hand to her face and wiped one eye and then the other with the heel of her hand.

The police would come of course. As soon as they found the body. Or rather the stolen bank card. Money stank more than bodies here. It raised hotels and lit the streets and slapped the smile onto everyone's face as they enjoyed their traditional Chinese holiday, and it created people like Meili and Ma Jun, who appeared like pebbles easing themselves out of the mud. For a little while. For every holidaymaker needs a happy time, and when happiness meant sex then Meili and Ma Jun obliged. For money, of course. "Industrialise Culture!" the four characters declared on every government brochure, "Raise the living standards yet higher!" And Meili had raised her skirts and hummed that tune many times, and she had raised her standing from hooker to hostess to mistress to murderer.

"What will happen to us?" Ma Jun asked that night as they lay on their money.

His head was pillowed on her shoulder. She shrugged. Care is wasted on things too far away, she remembered her grandmother saying as she knitted a face mask to keep out the winter pollution. It would take days for the police to find the body. Days, she thought and kissed Ma Jun's head.

But it had been days already. Three days in fact. And this was warm weather. The body would be starting to smell.

"They'll shoot us," she said, and kissed his head again, the back of his head, where the bullet would go in.

She had not been surprised when she fell for Ma Jun. She accepted it as natural, like turning the page of a book. It was what she had always been waiting for.

"I need some money," he said.

"Why?"

"I just need some money," he said.

She reached under the mattress and pulled out a wad of red hundred yuan notes, bundled together like lovers.

"We need fags," he said.

She watched him stand up and throw on his cheap suit jacket and walk out. She waited for him to return. An hour. Maybe more. And then something – a hair-fine edge of a wedge found the crack, and the crack opened like the tight curled fingers of a fist.

Ma Jun had stolen her money, she thought. Who needs two thousand yuan to buy a five yuan pack of cigarettes. The revelation was cold and chilling and she held it inside, quarantined it. He has gone to tell the police, she thought. He would be pardoned and she would be shot.

Meili stood up and pressed her skull to squeeze the thought out, but it was like trying to flatten a balloon; when she pressed one part the air forced itself into another. It was Ma Jun's suggestion to find a rich businessman. He dressed her in traditional Naxi clothes, with long silver earrings that flashed like fishing lures. They had caught Project Manager Mu's eye. He had the appeal of a wet toad. He was ideal. He was ugly and lonely and looking for someone to sleep with, and afterwards to listen. She poured his tea, laughed at his jokes and made him pay for her friend's meals.

Project Manager Mu smelt of money. It sweetened his breath, put a handsome light into his bespectacled eyes, and gave his chins a luxurious air, like a well-pillowed hotel bed. It even sweetened the memory of him afterwards, when she and Ma shared the money. But she had not given herself to him easily. It took a month of wooing for a brief copulation, and afterwards Project Manager Mu seemed unbearably guilty and happy all at the same time. Relieved, she thought later, as she and Ma counted the money.

Project Manager Mu had taken his wedding band off before he lay down with her, and when he had finished he put it back on. It was typical of him. She could picture him now, as he squeezed his ring back over his bloated knuckles.

Once he took his ring off and took her hand.

She pulled away. "What the hell are you doing?"

"I love you," he said.

She cradled her hand as if it was hurt.

"Show me."

Project Manager Mu gripped her again. "I can't bear to think of you doing this with anyone else."

"Doing what?"

His look took in the whole room, the deflated condom, the unkempt sheets. "This!" he said.

"Well!" she said, and turned her naked back on him.

"Be my second wife," he said.

She kept her back turned.

"Please."

She didn't give him an inch.

"How much do you want?" he said. "I will find a house for you. And nice clothes. And money as well. Twenty thousand. Enough? OK. Thirty thousand."

She gave in then, and was nice to him for as long as she could bear. Took his money for as long as she could bear. Was a second wife as long as she could shut the daylight out, the warmth from her skin, the music in her ears. And then one day, quite inexplicably she felt a desire to kill him. How could she resist? It was like needing to fart or sing. He was frightened as he died, and after she had killed him she saw that he had died without his wedding ring on.

It was there in his hand. She cleaned the blood away, and tried to get the ring back on, but his knuckles were too fat and the dead fingers too clumsy, and she got frustrated with him and flung the ring across the room, and then, a while later, as she was getting ready to leave, she noticed the ring lying against the bed leg and she picked it up and felt a thrill as she slipped it onto her middle finger. She would be his second wife, she thought, as she walked out that morning and felt the spring Lijiang sunlight on her face.

"When will they come?" Ma Jun asked that night, when he had come back with the fags.

"Who?" she said.

"The police."

Meili shrugged.

"Shouldn't we run away?" he said.

"Why? They'll catch us anyway." She kissed the back of his head again, and felt the fat wedding ring wrapped around her middle finger. "And then they'll shoot us."

"Will they shoot us together?" he asked after a while, as the end of the cigarette glowed briefly and dulled again.

"No," she said. "I don't think so."

But they'll cut our hearts out. And livers and kidneys.

She kissed his heart and his stomach, kissed his closed eyes, kissed the back of his head again.

"Will it hurt?"

"What?"

"Death."

Meili half laughed. She kissed his heart and stomach, kissed his closed eyes.

"Don't worry," she assured him. "It'll be fine."

THE ECONOMY OF VIOLENCE

KAY SEXTON

Kokuru was driving; Kokuru, squinting over the bonnet of the high truck, hissing at the pot-holes. He'd never lost anyone. That was his legend. Never lost anyone in the euphemistic sense; nobody had died in his care – nor in the literal one; none of his trucks or passengers had vanished into the veldt, rainforest, tundra, no man's land, dead zone, warehouse district, hinterland. It was supposed to be comforting. When he drove, you were safe. Except that safety's price was payable to Kokuru.

They were travelling back from Adhot. Or Sumah, or Bejgar, or Anhalj. From somewhere. Some god-neglected village on the outskirts of a hellhole. They were always villages, always miserable, as if the words village and misery were interchangeable, equating to universal misery in Caroline's mind.

Today she'd been auditing. Counting people in, food out. A translator asked each emaciated woman the same questions: how much rice, how much powdered milk, how much manioc, palm oil, sugar had she been given? Each man: how much millet, how much seed corn, how much kerosene? They all lied. The men, the women, the translator. So she weighed the sacks, weighed the words, weighed the reasons for deceit and created something, not a truth, but an approximate reality to account for it all. The women lied because the men beat them, the men lied because they owed the moneylender or the warlord, the translator lied because he owed money too, or his wife belonged to this village and she owed money, or his children had been taken away by the headman and he wouldn't see them again until the audit was done. Or he hated this village and wanted to punish the people. Or he lied because he could. So she taped the answers, to be translated once she returned to the field office. Even then, the translator's translator might lie, because he wanted more pay, like the ones who worked out in the field, or because he didn't speak the exact dialect of that village and was scared to admit it, or because he was being bribed to lie. So the tapes, and the transcripts, went back to headquarters in England and were translated again. The translator's, translator's, translator's translation.

She swayed, watching the violet horizon. The translator had been set down in his own village, so the truck was empty – just herself and Kokuru and the lies piling up where the sacks had been. Because it didn't end there. The administrators of Food For Peace had to sit down and decide: true lies or false lies? Good lies or bad lies? And, most of all, lies to tell the funders about, or not? Discoverable lies, or undiscoverable lies, that was the crux. If they were discoverable lies it was better to tell the funders and look transparent, but if they were undiscoverable, FFP risked losing funds because of its honesty. It was like living in a village. Do you tell a man his wife is cheating, and risk a beating for your honesty, or keep quiet and risk a beating when he finds out you knew?

Kokuru stopped the truck and turned off the ignition before looping his arms over the steering wheel. She gripped her seat. The price of safety. The waiting. Every time he drove, Kokuru stopped the truck if he was out at sunset. He'd seen the Green Flash once in his life and carried a photograph of it, cut from an astronomy magazine, in his wallet. 'Green Flash is not a myth,' he told everyone he drove. 'Many, many people think it's not true, but it is. You can see – if you are lucky and careful.'

It was a lie. Another lie. Kokuru watched for the Green Flash because when the sun set he made the roads safe for FFP. That was the price. The best driver FFP possessed was a man who could drive anywhere, his dark face impassive in the cold and calm in the heat – a cipher with a freak event as his talisman. She wished she was with one of the others; the Swiss driver called

Toblerone, the Greek one known as Atlas, or the bearded Welsh driver, nicknamed Phyllis for reasons nobody remembered.

The sun bellied down the horizon. Caroline wiped her face and buttoned her shirt. It could get cold in the dark.

Tonight it was her turn to pay. She tried to count up the times she'd waited with Kokuru but could only produce countries; Niger, Bosnia, Eritrea, Somalia. This wasn't the first time she'd travelled alone with him. In Sri Lanka they'd waited for the Green Flash that never came, and then he'd driven down from the mountain village to a plantation hut where he'd pulled three boys from their sleep and held a gun to the smallest's head until the other two began unwrapping landmines from sacks around the walls. She'd stopped him, made him hand them boys over. FFP hadn't even been in a war zone – it was drought relief food they were delivering. She'd stared him down, showing her contempt for his form of justice, and her glare hadn't wavered until the police turned up two hours later. The price had remained ahead of her then. It was right ahead of her now.

Kokuru pressed his chin on top of the steering wheel. She began to count on her fingers, knotting them under her shirt as though weaving a basket over her stomach. In Mogadishu they hadn't seen the Green Flash in three months, in Ibetu they'd spent a month of sunsets and seen nothing, in Mostar they'd only watched for five nights before they were pulled out of the combat zone, in Tsorena he didn't even bother.

'Why didn't we look for the Green Flash in Tsorena?'

Her voice was shrill. Kokuru spoke without lifting his chin, so his head moved up and down like a puppet's.

'You need low, far away horizon – don't get that in the mountains.'

The sun was gone, below the land. This was when the flash might appear, a momentary green glow caused by some freak atmospheric conditions Caroline didn't understand. Despite her fear, she began to rise in her seat, pushing up as the sun slid down, watching for the moment, the green blink, the instant of beauty.

Kokuru sighed – the moment had passed without reward.

Now the sky was the unlimited African purple that lived for a while before the stars punched through. Sometimes they throbbed until Caroline thought she could feel their heat. It caught her out all the time, that African blaze, so she stepped out into what looked like tropic warmth and found instead the chill of the highlands biting through her clothes.

Kokuru pointed at a small kerosene-lit shop, a mile or so up the road. 'You drive up there.'

She didn't want to look at him. She was supposed to ask what he planned to do and stop him, the way she had with the boys in Sri Lanka, but this was the price. This was what Kokuru did – the secret nobody discussed; the truth they all lied about. The price you paid, if you travelled with Kokuru was that eventually you must share in it. Making safe. Protecting. If you didn't, you weren't part of the deal, you didn't understand, you hadn't been made to pay. Kokuru kept FFP safe wherever he went, and you, whoever you were – auditor, translator, mediator, doctor, nurse, teacher, landmine-clearer – you paid his price.

He opened the driver's door and she slid across the bench seat. 'Count hundred-fifty then drive. Lights on. Stop outside. Okay?'

She nodded. The stars began to blurt through the dark, shoving the purple aside. The moon was thin. She counted on her fingers, tapping them against the steering wheel, then started the engine and turned on the lights, driving slowly forwards until the truck was outside the shop. She turned off the engine and scooted back to her own seat.

There was a sound she couldn't identify even afterwards, a roar or a bellow or an engine fighting its gears – not a human sound, although later she knew it must have been.

A man swarmed up the front of the truck, his arm upraised. She saw the panga in the starlight, the arc of it dividing the air. It pierced the truck bonnet a yard from her face. The blade and the truck screamed a metal duet and then he was hanging onto the knife with one hand, swinging his legs round, his feet in old training shoes aimed at the windscreen. He intended to kick his way into the cab.

She screamed.

She reached out, trying to find the door handle without looking away from the dark body hurtling over the metal towards her. Kokuru was standing by the door, holding it closed so she couldn't get out – his eyes on the man whose heels almost touched the glass. He raised his body onto the running board and leaned over, pressing the gun against the man's head.

He died.

The gun beneath the ear, angled up. The uneven spurt of brains from the exit wound, hardly seeming to rise before falling on the surface of the truck. The instant suppression of all that was human in the dark face beyond the feet. Death evident before the blood came, tar-coloured in the starlight.

Kokuru grabbed the body as it fell, hoisting it by a handful of shirt to the side of the road. He climbed the running board again to tug the panga free, metal screeching. He turned the blade in his hand, made experimental motions with his arm like a man cutting cane, and tucked it into his belt as he settled into the cab.

'He was waiting to hijack, not too smart, his plan. Two radio and four can gasoline in the shop. He got militia codes up on his wall, uh.'

She heard the affirmative, the 'uh' that said Kokuru had been right and this man with two radios was – had been – a spy, a profiteer, had planned their murder. He would have killed her and Kokuru too, buried them in a field, stolen the truck, sold it over the border, denied ever seeing them. And somehow Kokuru had known.

'Uh,' she said. Kokuru sat, jiggling the keys in the ignition. 'Uh,' she said louder. Yes, he had been right. Yes, he had saved them. Yes, the price was paid.

Kokuru nodded. 'Good he don't have both hands, uh. Or we'd 'a been in trouble.'

Caroline looked at the body as they drove past. The man's left hand was missing; the stump showed the clean excision of an old panga cut. She turned in her seat, first to the body, then to Kokuru. 'But that means he was a victim, he must have been in the genocide, he'd been mutilated...' He was

43

part of their work, was what she meant. The reason for FFP being there.

Kokuru shrugged, eyes on the road. He drove with the lights off uphill, using them only downhill, trusting moonlight to reveal the path wherever possible. Aid-worker symbols didn't help here. The best defence against attack was a truck with the lights off, collecting who knew whom, and taking them who knew where? People didn't lift their eyes to a dark truck, in case they found themselves inside it, answering the questions nobody dared to ask.

'You know what Kokuru mean?' His voice was cold.

Caroline shook her head, keeping her eyes on the gash in the bonnet.

'Means the city that didn't get atomic bomb. Kokuru City have cloudy sky that day. Hiroshima not so lucky. I think we were lucky today, Green Flash lucky.'

She nodded, not looking at him, counting on her fingers how many miles they were from safety.

GUS

DREW GUMMERSON

I have just moved into an apartment. It is on the top floor of a new block on a new development. On the first night I open the French doors and lean out over the railings. Across a patch of wasteland is the M1. I can see the lights strung out like lobster pots on a Greek sea. Below them the traffic vrooms, everyone going somewhere.

At the house-warming party we have cocktails. We are pressed together in the lounge. If you sit on the sofa and put your feet out you can rest them on top of the TV. Someone jokes that it is not really a 'house' at all and I go into the kitchen and find my boyfriend there. He has his hand down the back of another man's underpants.

"This is Gus," he says to me. "Gus is an ex Navy Seal."

I don't remember inviting any Gus and he is the kind of person you would remember. He is about six foot four and has a shaved head. On his left bicep is tattooed, 'In America We Trust'. His bicep is so big the words don't even fit halfway around.

My boyfriend passes Gus a bright blue cocktail in a glass the shape of an upside-down pyramid and pulls me to one side.

"I hope you don't mind, I've said Gus can stay here tonight."

"Can't he stay at your place?"

"I've got the boys coming over. It's a Wednesday. Wednesday is poker night. You know that. In fact..." my boyfriend looks at his watch, "I better shoot off. I'll call you tomorrow."

In the morning I wake up and know it's going to be one of

those days when the hangover never lets go. I pull back the duvet and stumble into the bathroom. Gus is in there. He is sitting on the toilet and he is naked. That makes two of us. I am naked too.

"Morning," says Gus. He has a deep Southern accent. "I don't know about you but I slept like a log. 'Preciate you lettin' me stay here."

"No worries," I say and walk out of the bathroom backwards.

There is no answer on either my boyfriend's landline or mobile so at one o'clock I take the bus into the city and walk the rest of the way to his house. This area has recently been taken over by Poles. My boyfriend is happy about this and often I will turn up to find his house full of these new immigrants, drinking beer on the stairs, talking poetry in the kitchen. Today the door is answered by Steve. Steve is his best mate, not Polish, more oafish.

My boyfriend and the rest of the poker crew, as he likes to call them, are all in the lounge. There are pizza boxes strewn across the floor, overflowing ashtrays, and the whole place stinks. They are sitting in front of the TV. On it is *The Sound of Music*.

"About this Gus?" I say.

My boyfriend puts a finger to his lips. "Shh. This is a good bit."

On the screen Julie Andrews comes running over the crest of a hill and starts to spin.

"Look," I say, "can we talk?"

My boyfriend leans forward and takes a piece of pizza from one of the boxes. It is the last piece and it looks like it's been there all night. There is a stubbed out cigarette next to it and a line of ash. He puts his head back and pushes the pizza into his mouth.

"Ever since you've moved into that flat," he says, mouth full, "you've been putting on airs and graces."

"I've been there four days. And I've only seen you once. That was at the party last night."

46

Steve slides down off the sofa and punches my boyfriend on the arm. "Oi, you git! Was that the last bit of pizza?"

"Finders keepers," says my boyfriend.

Steve puts an arm around my boyfriend and wrestles him on to his front. He then sits squarely on his back, yanks down my boyfriend's jeans, leans forwards, and blows a raspberry on his naked bum.

My boyfriend twists his head up and looks at me. "To be honest, I think I need a bit of space. I'm not sure me and you are working any more. You've got to realise there's a big world out there. Tell you what, call me in a couple of weeks."

Back at the flat Gus is sitting in the lounge and is poring over a map. On the table next to the map is a compass.

As I come in Gus looks up. "Give me ten," he says.

"Ten what?" I say.

I am thinking perhaps ten minutes and I am about to go into my bedroom to sit quietly on the bed when Gus stands, picks up the table to clear a space, and does ten press-ups.

"Ten," he says.

Ten is easy. I do them and wander through into the kitchen. I open a few cupboards. "Would you like something to eat?"

"Hey," says Gus, "you're pretty fit."

"Pasta?" I say.

We eat sitting in the lounge with the plates on our knees. There is nowhere else to eat as Gus's stuff is taking up pretty much the whole table. As Gus finishes he licks the plate clean and hands it to me.

"That was swell."

While doing the washing up I feel Gus is perhaps taking advantage. I've heard of this so-called American hospitality but it's not as if me and Gus really know each other. I dry the plates and march into the lounge.

Gus has cleared away the map and compass. Now he has some kind of weapon across his knees. Lined up on the table, standing on their blunt ends, are a number of bullets.

"You see these bullets," says Gus; "they are somewhat experimental, strictly under the counter." He picks one up and slides it into what appears to be the handle of the weapon. "They're made of four kinds of metal. They can pierce armour but if they enter the human body the metal flattens."

Gus narrows his eyes.

"One time in Iraq, I was on regular patrol, Sadr City, when rat-a-tat-tat the car was hit. One of my buddies was shot in the eye. Dead. I smashed out the window and fired. Bang. Hit this guy. We went to investigate. He was still twittering. The bullet had caught him in the left ass cheek, then done its stuff. It had taken his ass clean off. After that the other guys called me the Ass-Destroyer."

Gus holds one of the bullets up to the light. He squints his eyes, examines it, and slides it into the gun.

"That was before I got disillusioned with the whole thing. I was thinking. Last night was pretty uncomfortable on the sofa. While you were gone I checked the place out. I notice you got a pretty big bed. If you don't mind, tonight, I'll share with you."

As he says this Gus gives this big grin. That's probably the most dangerous thing about him. The grin is both goofy and sweet at the same time.

At some point in the night I feel something poking me in the ribs and fear the worst. I open my eyes and turn around. The bedroom light is on. Gus is sitting up on an elbow. Over his shoulder the alarm clock reads, '03:00'.

"Picture this," says Gus. "Go on. Close your eyes."

I think, just a few moments ago they were closed. I was asleep then.

"I dream of a world where we all live in harmony," says Gus. "Kind of like Eden, Adam and Eve and the snake and all that. People aren't oppressed there and it doesn't matter which God you believe in. You get me?"

I nod my head.

"There's a big lake," says Gus. "And it's always hot. And there's always apple pie. Sport is always on the TV and everyone has enough money to buy food. You see it?"

I say that I can and ask if I can go back to sleep now.

"I've come by this in-for-mat-ion," says Gus. That is how he says it, dragging out the syllables like a sack of coal being pulled down the stairs. "It's pretty dangerous stuff. I wonder if you would help me?"

He gives me that grin again, the one that is part goofy and the other part homespun cowboy. I think I say yes because of that. Or it might be because he has a very large gun.

In the morning I find the bed empty. Well, except for me. I am in it. I look at the clock. It is nine o'clock. I go through into the kitchen. Gus high fives me and slides a plate across the counter. It has omelette on it and some kind of fried potatoes.

"Get that down you," he says. "We've got a big day."

I guess this has to do with the 'in-for-mat-ion'. As I eat I watch Gus pack the maps and the gun and the compass into a black shoulder bag.

"Should I wear anything special?" I ask.

"Just act normal. What we have on our side is surprise."

He's right there. I haven't got a clue. I almost expect there to be a tank or a squad of compadres outside but we stand at the bus stop like normal people. Some of the local youths give Gus this look. I know what they mean. Gus seems to be many things all at once.

Gus keeps his eyes glued to the window during the journey, but we don't get off until the bus terminates in the city centre. We skirt past the Goths and skateboarders draped around the clock tower and head towards New Walk. The streets are filled with the usual shoppers going about their regular business. War, I always thought, was something that happened someplace else or in the movies. Gus makes me doubt that. Outside McDonalds a street seller approaches us shouting 'Big Issue, Big Issue', and I sense Gus tensing.

"It's just a magazine," I whisper. "Don't worry, we haven't been rumbled. Where are we going?"

"This way," says Gus.

At the top of Market Street the shoppers thin out and before us is the imposing edifice of the council building. I imagine we are going there, that being a place of in-for-mat-ion, but then Gus looks both ways, nips quickly to the left and ducks through the doors of the Leicester Central Lending Library. I click through the turnstile and eventually find him skulking by the autobiographies. He puts a finger to his lips.

"You heard in the press," he whispers, "about the CIA using holding cells on European soil?"

"I..."

"Shh," shouts a librarian from the front desk. He has a goatee beard and hair in a bun.

"This way," whispers Gus. "Act like you're looking for a book. Remember, they are not expecting us."

We go down a staircase to the basement. The silence is more absolute here, the smell from the books mustier. There is an old man in a plastic mac and a deerstalker hat. He is holding a travel book, *Chile by Night*.

We go to the end of one aisle and take a right. We go to the end of another. It becomes dimmer, the light above not working, or perhaps deliberately removed. Books crowd in on all sides like strangers in a packed subway carriage. At the end of one particular row we come to a space between the books and here is a door. It is almost perfectly hidden. You would only come across it by chance if you were looking for a book on mediaeval penis coverings, or other related subjects. The door has a sign with 'Private' written on it in crooked writing.

Gus puts one of his massive shoulders against it; there is a splintering sound and he is inside.

"What are you doing?" I hiss, but Gus has already gone.

On the other side of the door is a staircase. The steps are concrete, the handrail a painted white metal. It is lit from above by a single bulb.

"The thing about the CIA," says Gus, "is that they have their fingers everywhere. They are also deadly. Just do as I say and you won't get hurt. I am trained for this kind of thing."

We go down one level to a landing, and there is another bulb and another set of stairs going down. We do this five times, each staircase exactly the same as the one before but further underground. I have this sense of the world above me, but also another world, a hidden one, far below the surface.

50

At last we reach a final door with no more staircases. This is my last chance, I think. I could turn back now. But I don't. That's the thing about life; it's not about the big picture, it's about the individual choices you make along the way. And if I went back, what then? Would I always wonder what was behind that door?

Gus puts his ear against it and then steps back.

"Remember," he says. "This is for my dream."

He unzips a pocket on the front of his rucksack and takes out a putty-like substance. He presses this against the handle of the door in a neat pyramid and tells me to move away and put my fingers in my ears. Then he pushes a button on a black device he has in his hands. There is a pouff of noise and a cloud of dust and the door swings open.

What happens next happens very quickly.

Behind the door is a room. It has steel walls that shimmer in the bright fluorescent light from the ceiling. In the centre of the room is a table and on either side of the table is a man. They both have the same sharp suits, slick hair and pallid skin from either being underground too long or drinking too much cheap vodka.

They are already on the move as Gus leaps into the room. Perhaps they are scrabbling for guns or an emergency activation button. I'll never know. Gus catches the left-hand one with the flat of his foot in the stomach. The man crumples like two ends of paper set alight and emits a dull wheeze.

The second one Gus dispenses with a fist. The sound is like when I went to a fish restaurant and had to crack a lobster's claw with a large metal device.

"While I secure the perimeter," whispers Gus, "can you go and rescue the scientists?"

I don't know why he is whispering, not after the explosion. "What scientists?" I say.

Gus nods. "Through there."

I hadn't noticed the other door. I put my hand on the handle and finding it unlocked, go in.

This room is some kind of workshop. Shelves line the walls and they are filled with component after component after component; large screws, computer circuit boards, metal handles, glass jars full of tiny parts. The shelves seem to stretch up as far as I can see, with lamps clipped to them at odd angles, sending the light skittering in every direction.

In one corner are bunk beds, neatly made, and in another a toilet and shower cubicle divided from the rest of the room by a thin curtain. But dominating the scene, in the centre of the workshop, is a contraption. It is like one of those car games you can actually sit in at the seaside, except that it is not finished. One side is sleek and functional, metal panels gleaming and a kind of door, but the other is a mass of wires and tubes in every colour you could imagine, sticking out, waiting to be connected to something. Standing by the side of this are two more men. These must be the scientists.

The men have skin the colour of baked sand. They have neat square-cut beards. Each is holding a spanner.

"Hello," I say. "We've come to rescue you."

They both bow their heads. "Thank you. Allah Akbar."

At the top of the final staircase, just as we close the door marked 'Private' behind us, we are approached by that librarian with his hair in a bun and the goatee beard.

"There was talk of a disturbance," he says, eyeing us suspiciously. "Did you find everything you were looking for?"

"Ah here it is," says Gus and pulls a book off a shelf. "Sometimes something can be right under your nose and you can't see it."

No doubt this is ironic. The two scientists are standing behind Gus in a line, hidden from view by his massive body.

Back at my flat, in the kitchen, I pull Gus to one side.

"They can't stay here." The scientists are sitting side by side on the sofa, knees almost pressed against the TV. "There's not enough space."

"They can have the spare room," says Gus. "We can make it into a kind of dormitory workshop fusion. You and I are quite settled in your bed already."

"We've spent one night together."

"That's what I mean," says Gus. "Settled." He gives me that grin again.

Over the next few weeks the scientists spend most of the time in their room. Sometimes they go out and come back with objects, the bumper of a car, a box of fuses, a piece of plate glass. They don't speak much, or say where they go yet somehow we get along. Even the noise from their room doesn't bother me. There is something rhythmical about the tapping, or the hammering. Sometimes it will go on late into the night and one morning I am woken by what sounds like loud clapping and a spontaneous cheer. It is four a.m.

I have the sense that something important is happening. I'd seen all that stuff about Iraq on the TV at the time. You couldn't miss it. But now a piece of Iraq had come to me and I liked it. I couldn't explain any more than that. Or perhaps I could, it was like Gus's dream, everyone getting along.

One day I disturb one of them in the bathroom combing his beard. For a moment he seems embarrassed and then he smiles broadly.

"Six months I spent in hole," he says, "then you bring me here. It is very nice place. Verrrry nice." The way he rolls his r is soft and warm and somehow makes me feel proud.

In the evenings while eating dinner we watch TV. The scientists like cartoons the most and sit laughing like drains at *Bugs Bunny*, *Road Runner*, *Hong Kong Phooey*. It is summer so I open the French doors. If the wind is in the right direction we can hear the traffic on the M1. The lorries make the most noise. Sometimes if there is a particularly loud lorry the scientists will throw themselves down onto the floor and put their hands over their heads. But life goes on and Gus and the scientists are part of my life now.

Towards the end of September Gus and I are sitting on my bed, a Scrabble board between us, when there is a knock at the bedroom door. I shout 'come in' and the two scientists are there grinning like idiots.

"We finish," they say. "Come see."

Strange as it may seem, as it is my flat, I haven't been in their room before. Under the window are two narrow cot beds and on all the walls are shelves crammed with part after part after part. I am reminded of that workshop below the library, especially as in the centre of the room is that machine again, the one I thought looked like a sit-in car game at an amusement arcade. Only now it is finished.

Wacky Races is another of the cartoons that has been on over the summer and one of the scientists' favourites. The object in front of me looks something like Dick Dastardly and Muttley's Mean Machine. It is coloured a bright purple, there is a glass bubble dome, a series of wheels, and inside thousands of switches. That's what I remember the most, all those switches. They are everywhere.

"What is it?" I ask.

"It's time machine," says one of the scientists. "Iraq was before Mesopotamia, birthplace of civilisation, you see?"

"Things very good then," says the second scientist. "All beautiful and words so beautiful. You want try?"

I look at Gus. I realise we are both naked. This is our habit recently, to play Scrabble naked in the mornings.

"Not now," I say. "We've got a game to finish."

"Yep," says Gus and he puts a hand on my shoulder. "But give us a buzz when you get back. If you do."

"Okey-dokey," say the scientists. "Yes, we will."

We go back into our room. As we sit back down on the bed the whole flat is gripped by a violent shaking. Books dislodge themselves off the shelf and fall to the floor. From the kitchen there are the sounds of glasses breaking. Then there is a loud bang like a glass vacuum being burst, quickly followed by a high pitched whizzing noise.

"That'll be them gone then," says Gus. "Mesopotamia, the birthplace of civilisation and all that."

"Is it my turn?" I say and smile.

Quite amazingly the scrabble board on the bed is undisturbed, the vibrations perhaps absorbed by the thick duvet. I put some tiles down in a neat line and score one hundred and six points with the word 'quasar'.

HOW BHOOMI BROKE HER BONDS

SHARON MAAS

No sign of Bhoomi when Aditi returned from the school run; hopefully, jetlag would keep her in bed half the day, delaying her own duties as gracious hostess. She cleared away the breakfast table, washed the dishes, made the beds, and went down to the backyard to tend the roses. The morning was gorgeous; a hummingbird hovered above the bougainvilleas, wings aflutter; kiskadees played and called up in the mango tree; and best of all, the bottom house was wrapped in silence. Bhoomi still slept.

What had she been thinking, importing this woman from India, sight unseen? Bhoomi was the last person to bring Indian Culture to British Guiana. But then again, there hadn't been much choice; teachers of Classical Indian Dancing weren't exactly standing in line to come halfway across the world. She'd taken the first best applicant with not even a photograph, much less an interview; the only applicant, in fact. Now she was stuck with Bhoomi, a husband-hunter.

"EEEEEEEEEEEEEEEEEEEEEIAAAA!"

The piercing shriek, quivering with panic, tore through the morning idyll, the Psycho scream of a woman at knife's edge. Aditi dropped the rose basket and raced to the bottom house. She pounded on Bhoomi's door.

"Bhoomi, let me in… What's the matter?"

The door flew open. Bhoomi fell into Aditi's arms in yesterday's slept-in sari, now hanging crumpled on her tiny frame in dishevelled loops. Her hair was wild as a sensa fowl's forward-growing feathers, her face, smudged with last night's make-up, convulsed in a mask of terror.

"A man!" she shrieked. "Looking in my window! A *black* man! A *Negro!*"

"What? Let me see!" Aditi ran to the window and looked out. No man, black or otherwise, in sight. She ran outside and glimpsed a somewhat familiar form slipping between the bougainvilleas.

"You there! Come out!"

The man stopped, turned and stepped forward, head hanging. His short, ragged trousers and a torn, grubby singlet did little to cover his dark lithe body. He looked up at Aditi, eyes clouded with guilt.

"Oh, Errol! It's *you!*" Aditi sighed in relief, frowned and tried to look cross, an art she'd never quite managed, not even with her children. "Did you look into Bhoomi's window?"

Errol's fingers fidgeted with a silver name-chain on his wrist, and he scratched one taut brown calf with a bare and calloused foot.

"Aunty, ah too sorry. Ah din' know somebody livin' dere already. Ah din' mean no harm, ah just peep inside curious-like, to see if de painting an' such finish."

Which was his good right, Aditi thought, seeing as he'd built the room himself. He'd done a good job too; the floor was flat and the door handle was the right way up, details she didn't take for granted.

"Well, you scared the living daylights out of my guest. So keep away from her. Go and start work."

"All right, Aunty." Errol beamed, and she smiled back, for his grin was infectious. She watched as he swung off to work, then reluctantly returned to Bhoomi's door, now closed again, and knocked once more. Bhoomi opened it a crack, peering out as if expecting an ambush.

Aditi put on her most welcoming smile. "Well, good morning, Bhoomi, and sorry for the rude awakening! It was only the carpenter. He meant no harm."

"I was *terrified!* Imagine waking up, suspecting nothing, and a black face is peering at you through the window!"

"Yes. It must be shocking to see *any* face peering in at you through the window! I do apologize for Errol. I'll make him come and apologize himself..."

Bhoomi shrieked, covering her mouth with her hand.

"Oh *no!* I am not wanting to even see him *ever* again! What if I had been *naked* on the bed!"

"He's hardly an axe-murderer on the rampage! It's my fault entirely. I should have drawn the curtains last night. And I had these specially made, to match the paint. Aren't they pretty?" Aditi walked over to the curtains and held them up for inspection, but Bhoomi refused to be distracted.

"Has he gone now? Is he working here every day?"

"Now and again. He's building a garden shed. It's going to take a few days, I'm afraid."

"But how can I take bath with a man walking around outside. What if he peeps in the window again!"

"He won't. And can't; I just drew the curtains. And the bathroom window is milk-glass. But I tell you what, Bhoomi. Come upstairs. Bring your clean clothes; today you can shower in the family bathroom."

"But I would have to go outside – he might see me! How embarrassing!"

"We'll use the front stairs; he's in the backyard."

"I will wrap the bed sheet around me!" Bhoomi said. "Oh! What a fright! I almost had a heart attack." She lowered her voice. "I didn't even know you had them in this country. My sister didn't mention them at all. She said this place was Little India, a Hindu village halfway across the globe. I wish she'd warned me the place is swarming with Negroes. And it really is behind God's back. I never..."

"You'll get used to it," Aditi said stiffly. "If you decide to stay."

Bhoomi pinched her lips together. "Well – let's go up then. Just let me find a sari."

She delved through her suitcase, lifting up a variety of saris in different fabrics and colours. Aditi stood watching. The contents of the valise engulfed her in nostalgia. The rustle of silk, the rich colours, the very smell that wafted out of the folded clothes – all was suffused with the breath of India, a country enclosed in a suitcase. She felt a pang of homesickness, but pressed it away, far from her.

"I am ready", said Bhoomi. "But you go first, just in case. You never can tell with those men. They hide in the bushes to peep at us ladies. Especially unmarried ladies and widows like myself are at risk."

"I assure you he's not peeping." Aditi was already exhausted; she longed to get Bhoomi into the shower, out of sight and hearing. "Just follow me." She strode briskly out of the room and over to the front stairs. Bhoomi scuttled behind her, wrapped up in a sheet.

Bhoomi had a shopping list, Tamil lettering on a tiny scrap of paper folded into a knob and tucked into her bra. In particular, she wanted fabrics.

Walking over to Bookers, Aditi now felt tender and protective. Look at how Bhoomi scuttled to keep up, panting, clutching her handbag! One should be indulgent towards such a small person, and forgiving. Life could not have been easy as a widow in India; this was her big chance; chance for a career and even, as Bhoomi had hinted last night, at marriage, her final goal. There was no prejudice against Hindu widows here. Aditi slowed her brisk stride and smiled down at Bhoomi, who beamed back up through her mask of caked white face-powder.

Today Bhoomi wore a poison-green sari, bulky where she had bunched the excess length into the petticoat's waistband, and swishing around her twinkling feet, making her rather egg-shaped.

While they were inspecting the fabrics Aditi felt a firm tap on her shoulder,

"Good morning Aditi," said a disembodied voice.

Aditi swung around.

"Yasoda Aunty! What a surprise! This is Bhoomi."

She pushed Bhoomi forward. Yasoda, tall and skinny, peered down, and did namaste.

Bhoomi did namaste back, explaining, as she'd done last

night at the airport, first thing, "I'm not a dwarf, I'm only very short."

"Achha, so you're the new Dancing Teacher! Everyone has been talking about you; this country is like a village. How are you enjoying your stay?"

Bhoomi's little white face beamed up at Yasoda.

"Very nice, thank you! We came here to purchase some fabric. But we are having a little problem – this here is bad quality." She waved towards the piled-up bolts of cloth in contempt, dismissing them all.

Yasoda shook her head, wrinkled her nose and hawked without spitting. Aditi longed to flush out her throat with a large syringe.

"This is the African store," Yasoda said. "You must go to the Indian stores – the sari shops. They are all in Regent Street. Sanjay's Sari Emporium, Kirpilani's. They have just brought in some new artificial silk. All the goods are imported from India. Aditi, you must take her there immediately. Or would you allow me to escort you? Shall I take you under my wing? Aditi, is that all right?"

Aditi felt Yasoda's beady eyes looking straight through her.

"Ask her yourself," she said stiffly. "She is an adult woman, not a child."

"I look young but I am twenty-five!" Bhoomi said, nodding.

Yasoda smiled fondly down at Bhoomi – who beamed up like a small child in front of Santa Claus – and proffered a bony elbow.

"Hook me, my dear," she said, and the next minute she and Bhoomi, arm in arm, tall and small, a green sari and an orange one, walked out of Bookers together. Aditi gazed after them.

Well, if that's the way it is, she thought, *Bhoomi might as well move in with Aunt Yasoda.*

Which, two weeks later, she did. And good riddance.

Yasoda heard the sirens in her sleep, and someone screaming "Fire!" Blinking red lights flashed across the room; more sirens drawing closer, shouts from the street below, loud banging on the downstairs door

She scrambled out from beneath the mosquito net and ran to the window. Two fire-engines, lights flashing, sirens wailing, stood on the street; a crowd of people, firefighters unrolling a length of hose, shouting, pointing, a hubbub of excitement. Flames whipped from the windows of the house next door, a two-storey Dutch-colonial house. Like her own home, wooden. Fire Fodder.

Retribution Mary lived there with her husband, a meek, mild Registrar of Deeds. Mary was a Georgetown icon. She walked the streets beating on a saucepan and screaming "Retribution! The Lord is nigh!" Or she stood on the bridge with dishevelled hair accosting the passing women: "Ah gon buy yuh a new panty. Yuh panty stink." And to men: "Ah gon cut off yuh cock. It shrivel up."

Yasoda ran down the corridor. At Bhoomi's door she stopped and hammered at it, screaming: "Bhoomi, fire, wake up, run!" She rattled the handle, but of course the door was locked; Bhoomi kept it that way for fear of random rapists, when she was inside the room, or random burglars, when she was outside it.

No response; Bhoomi was a sound sleeper. Yasoda battered on the door again, screamed Bhoomi's name, hesitated a moment wondering where the axe was, then, in total panic, raced downstairs.

Outside on the road she looked around, frantic for help. The firemen were all busy with the burning house. A third fire-engine approached; Yasoda ran to it.

"There's someone still in there!" she shouted to the driver, and pointed to Bhoomi's open window. Flames were already leaping across from next door.

"We'll get her," the fireman said calmly. The fire-engine crawled up to the house and a ladder edged its way up to Bhoomi's window. When it was fully extended a big, black fireman began the ascent.

Even in the midst of her panic Yasoda wanted to call him back and request an *Indian* fireman – but it was too late. He was already halfway up.

Terror rose in her gorge as a lump of putrid phlegm. She

hawked – once, twice, thrice, each time more violently than before. The third attempt dislodged the phlegm. It shot it upwards and slithered onto her tongue, thick and nasty-tasting. She spat; it arched before her and fell to the road, shiny and yellow in the fire's glare.

A curtain in one of the side windows had caught fire; a firefighter turned his hose on it. The crowd had grown, neighbours coming to ogle. Retribution Mary, wrapped in a sheet, stood with her husband shouting, "The Day of Retribution has come! Praise the Lord!"

The swelling crowd engulfed Yasoda, pushed her forward against the barrier set up by the firefighters. Her face felt roasted, and naked. Her nylon nighty clung to her body and singed her skin. She gazed up at Bhoomi's window as the fireman climbed through, impatient for his re-emergence with Bhoomi over his shoulder. *Thank goodness she is so small,* she thought. *She is as light as a feather, like a child. And he looked big and strong. I hope she doesn't struggle too much.* Red flames or black firefighter: what a choice for Bhoomi!

The fireman appeared at her elbow, seemingly out of nowhere. "De room empty, ma'am!" he said.

"Of course it wasn't empty! Did you look properly? Under the bed?"

"Yes, ma'am. Empty. So I break down de door and search de house. Nobody inside. She must be come out before you. Excuse me." He touched his helmet and hastened off.

Yasoda frowned. Had Bhoomi woken up first and come down before her? She felt betrayed – why hadn't Bhoomi woken her, warned her? She elbowed through the throng looking for Bhoomi. The fire was under control now, but the air buzzed with excitement as spectators milled around hoping something terrible would happen.

Yasoda stopped fretting about Bhoomi's betrayal and began to worry. Where on earth was she?

A taxi drew up nearby, blowing its horn to clear a way through the milling crowd. It stopped, a door opened, and Bhoomi emerged, fully dressed, the inevitable handbag slung over one elbow. Yasoda hurried over.

"Bhoomi! Where have you been all night?" Yasoda's voice was that of a furious father reprimanding a wayward daughter. Bhoomi responded in kind.

"Oh, I, well, you see, I went, um, the thing is…"

"Tell me!"

"I couldn't sleep so I went for a drive…"

"At this time of night? Where to?"

"I needed some fresh air… I couldn't breathe… I couldn't sleep! So I went for a walk on the sea wall."

"Don't lie! Only choke-and-robbers and whores go walking on the sea wall at this hour. Tell me the truth!"

Instead of answering, Bhoomi opened her handbag and peered in. Nervous fingers fumbled in its depths, found what she was looking for, a little lace hanky.

"It's so terribly hot!" she cried, wiping her face. "Was there a fire?"

"You dropped something," said Yasoda, bending down.

She held up the thing, a man's silver name-chain, and peered at it, squinting in the fire-engine's still rotating light.

"Who's *Errol?*" She stepped forward, glaring at Bhoomi. Then frowned, and looked down. There was something under her bare foot, something soft and squishy. She lifted the foot and bent down to inspect its sole. A patch of thick yellow phlegm clung to it. Disgust washed through her.

"Bhoomi, give me that kerchief!"

When no answer came she looked up. Bhoomi was gone.

A car door slammed.

The taxi pulled away.

THE EXPERIMENT OF LIFE

JONATHAN HOLT

When we are thirty-two years of our age the landlady says we must leave the apartment because we wash clothes on Sunday one time and play our mood-like music too loud always. Uncle hears of this and says we must stay in his shop. We do not wish to be homeless or to return to the village where we came from in the more mountainous regions, so we tell Uncle we are thanking him for the offer.

Uncle is the big one-time furniture purveyor in Zurich. He is old – close to his rest. We are the only nephew and niece of his, and the son he has is dead from the avalanche. Uncle never gives generosity to us, and this makes us very glad to be having it.

The shop is little – small shop – and we are moving dusted furniture out of the stacks for two days to have the place to sit and to read or only to sleep. We use the long metal desk to hold the television on, but the other furniture from Uncle we move out. Behind this small shop there is the biggest room, very bright with the lights from the ceiling. Under the lights there are the kitchen parts that nobody wants to purchase and many, many toilets. One toilet is self-to-clean, and this one is attached to the sewage. We get used to it.

Uncle opens this shop first thing after he comes to Zurich in the year of 1956, and he keeps it when the business sells to the conglomerate. Too much sentimental baggage. According to us Uncle is the saddest man, even to spite the riches and the pampered white moustache, or because he has such riches and moustache. Father knows this also, we are certain for it. He visits Uncle for the Swiss National Day, to drink the Klosterbräu and talk to the memories of Grandmother and Grandfather at the fireside. Uncle makes Father bring the towel and the soap for himself from the village and pay half for the cost of the beer. He does this, according to us, because Father is the clergy.

When Uncle comes to eat dinner for our gratitude about the shop, first thing he does is to pull the shades down.

You cannot have these immigrants to look into here, he says at us. You do not know what they are making ready to do. They are dangerous. They have the bad smells and are absent of all these scruples.

In the apartments on this street where the shop is situated many, many immigrants are living. So many refugees are in Switzerland at this time because there is the war in Yugoslavia, and the government is asking for them to have houses. According to us, Uncle says we must live in the shop because the government says he must let the immigrants have it for the housing, because of the vacancy. The government is paying for this privilege but the people like Uncle are putting up the resistance to it. In *Die Weltwoche* a man writes his letter to complain. In his apartment building the playing room for the little children is taken for the immigrants to live in. His complaining is because the children must now play in the apartment of his psychotherapy practice. And there is the smell.

Uncle is cutting the steak when we tell him we are making the film about this life in the shop. Why could you think to do it, he says. He looks at us and stops the chewing to see which one is the speaker. We are twins. The only difference is because one of us is the boy and the other is the girl.

Where do you get the money, he also wants to know. Uncle thinks of everything as too expensive. He leaves for the Beethoven at the Tonhalle before we are able to pour him the schnapps.

First thing we do now is to pull the shades up. This is why we have the idea to make the film to begin on. We live the life of the produce, with the people on the street having the invitation to watch us with the dinner plates or the toenail clipper. This is the experiment of life.

We tape the video cameras onto the ceiling, one looking onto us in the shop, the other one looking onto the people in the window. It is not successful for the week or two because no one in the window has the desire to look at us and we cannot be interested in the tape when we see it because we know how it is to look like we are reading newspapers or having our food.

We are talking one night about putting the experiment to rest, but we do not do it so far. At the next afternoon we have the television on the EuroNews. This is the channel with only pictures of the travesties and wastes of the world over, no anchorman in the suit. We switch the sound off so we do not have to listen to the languages. When we look up from our food on the plates we see three immigrants looking in onto us from the glass.

At the first we cannot believe what we are doing to have this attention. We continue to eat the rösti and do not change to meet this behaviour. There are more immigrants eventually. There are the Swiss also, and one who is from Canada (there is the maple leaf on her shirt). They are watching the pictures on the EuroNews. There are the people in the graves and the mothers which are crying over them. There is the rubble. There is Bill Clinton at the White House with the flash bulbs all over him.

We get used to the attention.

At night time we are on the cushions reading the books of Nietzsche. It is the business of the very few to be independent, we say, it is the privilege of the strong. And we nod at this vast wisdom. The door of the shop opens. It is the very black African man we have seen to leave the building where the immigrants are resident.

Hallo, we say at him. He is nodding. He has the very serious look like the careful shopper. He looks around at the shop and moves himself to turn the pages of the heavy book of the Bauhaus movement on the table. After this he picks up the coconut shell and sniffs at it. He is smiling about it. He holds the coconut shell at his ear and moves his waists like he is the dancer of the Hawaiian party or at the Saturday night soiree at Lagos. He is the happy man of all Africa, and for this reason we do not say he must leave the shop.

He sees across more of the items of our possessions. His finger is between the layers of our sweaters on the shelf, but he does not raise any sweaters up at himself. Then he rests at the sofa and looks onto the television. It is the pictures of the bodies from the grave. These are the people of the people in the building where he is residing.

Very bad, he says, very bad. His head is shaking and he is looking like the undertaker. He smells like the spices and the – how do you say it – whale musk. This is the smell that we like. We are becoming used to the African man being in the shop.

We conduct the interview for the camera.

Why did you came to Switzerland, we ask him – like this. He is laughing at this. You are persecuted? They beat you with the sticks? They slaughter the children? He laughs still. You are homosexual? You know what this is, to be homosexual? He pulls his mouth together and is looking at us with very big anger, then he points his finger onto us and laughs. He laughs too far, not like the happy man again. This is something other.

Please, we say. Please. We motion onto the door with our hands. Two immigrants outside the glass stand with the tears flowing on the cheeks. The African is nodding his grin at us. He does not leave the shop. Instead of this he yawns and looks above us at the ceiling where there are the cameras. When there is the silence – long time silence – he lies himself across the sofa and closes his eyes until they are shut.

What can we do about it? We get used to it.

We switch off the light.

LAST RITES OF AN ENGLISH ROSE

PATSY ANTOINE

An amateur fisherman finds her torso during an early walk along the Thames. He arrives just as the first hints of day blot the night sky and as the city gently snores. At the edge of the water he pauses to enjoy the dawn reflecting on the lapping water, the streetlights blinking off on the opposite bank, early birds chirping an easy melody. That's when he sees it: a black bin bag half submerged in the water. It's probably rubbish, he thinks, but he's already imagining far worse. He drags it out of the water, pulls it open and gags. Next to the bloodied torso is a small, stained handbag.

★

A strong undercurrent pulls her downstream, tide and motion tugs at her, spins her in a ceremonial dance. After a time she floats gently on the surface, bobs past Big Ben, slides inconspicuously under Waterloo Bridge.

It is a cloudless night and a full moon sends light across the water's surface. The night is cold and so is the water, helping to keep decay at bay.

Her remains are helped into the water, of course: a tall, dark man with a chiselled mask for a face. He wears sunglasses in that conspicuously inconspicuous way, despite the darkness of a late night by the river, devoid of street lights. He wears forest green gardening gloves with red ribbed cuffs but his suit is a Boateng – an odd juxtaposition.

"Hurry, Yusuf," says Ben, his companion. A stocky, white man with a big head and severe halitosis. "We gotta finish this. You know the procedure…"

Yusuf lights a cigarette and inhales deeply. His hands are shaking and he draws hard on the cigarette to steady himself. He sighs. He can still see her face, fear etched into the skin there, the last image of her before he puts her severed head, legs and arms in a second bag. He liked her, felt a kindred spirit somehow. He already knows that her face will haunt him for a long time to come.

★

They bundle her roughly into the boot of the car in two black bin liners. The garage is dark but slithers of yellow light leak in from the street through small gaps in the wooden door. As Ben collects the plastic sheeting, Yusuf slips her clutch bag in with her torso, ties the bag securely and allows himself a smile. It's not much, but maybe it will be enough. Ben comes back, slips the stained plastic in the boot with her remains and the two men leave.

Yusuf is unusually quiet as he drives. He pushes in the car lighter and roots around in his pocket for a cigarette. When he finds one the lighter's orange glow shakes as he attempts to light it.

"Get a grip," says Ben. "You want out… I'll give you out." He pulls back his jacket. There is a knife stuck in his belt.

★

The man in the beaded veil slices easily through her flesh with his cutlass while his followers chant sacred words and sway like black flowers in the wind. When he cuts her legs the floor quickly becomes deep, raw red. He spins and spins and his coloured cloak flies up around him. He is dancing around her as a river of blood spreads from its mutilated host, a stream of glutinous liquid flowing across plastic. The chanting becomes louder, more urgent.

Yusuf watches silently. He no longer chants. The beaded veil is all that remains of a tradition warped by outsiders. Before bloodlust replaced ritual. Before he switched allegiance to a new, forbidden god. He remembers the way her halter-neck dress caressed the curve of her hip. The way her golden hair bounced at the turn of her head.

Now all he can see is red, her blood flying up as she is murdered. They still insist on calling this sacrifice. A traditional ritual that must happen. But there is nothing ritualistic about what they do here. In front of him the veiled man has slowed. The life in Rose's eyes has long since died and she stares at him from beyond consciousness, her face caught in a pained grimace.

Yusuf can almost taste the bile rising in him, can feel the food churning in his stomach as he remembers the conversation he shared with her not an hour before. The veiled man has stopped and is watching him. He points at Yusuf and gestures for him to come forward. When Yusuf is in front of him the veiled man lifts his cutlass and brings it down with force, severing Rose's head.

★

She is dizzy and feels disorientated. The wine is strong, but instinct tells her this is more than that. She tries to focus on finding the door, but the walls and ceiling blur and she loses balance. She hears a crack as her head hits the floor and somewhere nearby she hears a wine glass smash. The CD he put on earlier is still playing, some fella warbling over unfamiliar music. Her eyes are open. She can see him standing over her, but she can't move. Her heart is beating hard in her chest, echoing in her head and filling the space between her ears.

"I'm sorry," he whispers.

She tries to move, but the instructions from her brain refuse to reach her hands. Disorientated by the drug he's used clear thoughts became muddied; the room swirls around her and rushes round him. Yusuf leaves the room and she drifts in and out of consciousness. Another man enters. He is stocky and wears a five-pointed star on his chest. He leans over her and speaks unfamiliar words in a harsh language. His breath smells.

She hears a sound, a door opening and then there are people. People dressed in black. People chanting strange words over and over again. Fabric moves fluidly around the women as they surround her, their bare feet padding on the floor. And then the man in the beaded veil comes. Lines of tiny, colourful beads hang in front of his face and cover his head until they meet in a peak on his crown. As he moves the beads sway like a curtain in the breeze. But when they move she still can't see his face.

Her eyes dart to the painting on the wall and fear over-whelms her.

★

When she arrives he takes her straight to the lounge. The room is contemporary chic. Sleek metal wall units, black leather sofas, chrome ornaments, clean lines, bachelor pad charm. She likes what she sees. Strangely, the floor is lined with see-through plastic. On the wall a mahogany framed painting depicts an ancient tree, its branches hanging low over a village scene. Paint splashes create women wrapped in black cloth, their heads wrapped again with the same. They gather in a circle beneath the tree. In the middle a man lies awkwardly, his neck at an unnatural angle. In the circle someone is adorned in colourful fabric, head and face covered with an intricately beaded veil. He holds two machetes stained and dripping red. Around them straw dwellings dot the landscape and in small windows red eyes stare out at her.

"Like the painting," she says with a note of sarcasm in her voice.

"It reminds me of home," he says. He looks sleek in a tailored suit. He is charming, polite, distracted. "Wine?" he asks her.

She nods.

"Red okay...?"

She nods again and Yusuf disappears into the kitchen. "No

70

need for any fuss," she calls out to him, even though she's enjoying the attention. She is so tired of being alone.

"How long have you been in Soho?" he calls from the kitchen.

"Not long. It ain't exactly stimulating, but it's better than the other stuff. No offence, like…"

Yusuf comes back into the room carrying two glasses. "None taken," he says as he passes her a glass of red. He puts on a CD and tells her it's Fela.

She gulps from the glass and perches herself on the back of the sofa. He seems different from the punters she remembers back when she was on the game. She wonders how quickly she can make the front door if she needs to. "Nice place," she says. "I always wanted somewhere like this…"

"It does not come easy."

"Believe me, nothing comes easy…"

The ticking of the chrome clock on the wall fills the silence between them. "Before we begin I have cooked a meal," says Yusuf. "Please… relax…"

They eat a meal of seasoned rice and chicken in groundnut sauce, which he has cooked himself. She hasn't eaten so well in a long time. As the meal progresses he seems more chilled, less intense. She relaxes. He explains how he prepared the food, even though she shows little interest. He talks about the choice of wine, about his homeland, about feeling like an outsider.

"So, why some dried up old has-been like me?" she asks him when their scant conversation lulls.

"You looked sad."

She catches herself before the surprise shows on her face. "Any more wine?" she asks him, holding out her empty glass. When he comes back with a full glass they sit in silence over empty dinner plates.

She feels like she's being watched. Across the room red eyes gleam from the huts in the eerie village painting.

"I know the artist," says Yusuf, watching her. "I'll give you his card."

"People like me don't need artists…"

71

"No, I insist…" he says. He takes a card from his wallet and holds it out until she takes it from him.

She puts it in her clutch bag.

Yusuf smiles.

"Do you know what it feels like to be trapped?" she says.

For the first time since meeting him, Yusuf looks uncomfortable. He stares down at his plate, drains the last of his wine from its glass, then looks across the room at the village painting. When he responds his voice is wistful. "Yes… I think I do," he says.

★

She applies her make-up using the hostel's bathroom mirror. It's the most flattering. Her face was beautiful once, before forty-a-day carved crow's feet at her temples. But her watery blue eyes still sparkle with youth.

She chooses the red dress. It hugs her figure, enhances her curves and reveals her pale, lean back. She piles her hair high on her head then decides to wear it down so it softens and frames her face.

She takes the bus to central London, just another anonymous commuter. It's a warm Friday night and pubs spit smokers onto the surrounding pavements. She tunes into the city's pulse – the smell of Thai food is on the air; Poles share casual conversation on the bus; black and white youths waddle like penguins in low-slung jeans. She changes in Leicester Square and takes another bus out, following the Thames past Waterloo Bridge, Big Ben.

When she arrives, his road is calm suburbia.

She rings the doorbell. Fixes her hair while she waits, reapplies lipstick.

"Da da," she says when he opens the door, as if she's just done a magic trick.

Yusuf smiles and beckons her inside. "Hello, English Rose."

★

She is an ex-stripper who is paid to stand in a Soho doorway to lure punters inside. Life hasn't gone her way.

It is mid-afternoon but the street is still buzzing. People flit past her doorway and she catches snippets of foreign conversations on the wind. She is bored and tired, but knows nothing else. She moves outside of the doorway and lights up a cigarette. She has just inhaled deeply when he approaches.

"How much?" he says.

She's been on the game long enough to know what he's asking. She takes her time to exhale, the smoke escaping through her nostrils.

"It ain't that kind of place," she says, looking up and down the street. "But come in, take a look. I reckon you'll still like what you see."

"No," he says. "How much for you, later... you and me." His face is blank. When he speaks his voice is thick with accent.

She shrugs.

"What is your name?"

"Rosie," she says.

"Eh, eh... English Rose?" He says and laughs at his own crap joke.

He takes off his glasses and she is able to get a measure of him. He isn't the usual sort, with his shiny shoes, Diesel sunglasses and manicured nails. But there is something sad in his eyes.

"You have family, Rosie?" he says.

"None that give a damn," she replies.

"Two kola nuts together," he says and he smiles a sad smile.

She doesn't understand so draws on her cigarette, watching him watching her. When he leans in to whisper in her ear she can smell his cologne and the aroma stirs something in her groin.

He tells her an address and a time and quotes an absurdly generous fee.

She knows she won't be able to resist.

CHANGING REELS

MATT THORNE

Reel 2

No matter where he is in the world, Michael Chambers always tries to get to bed half an hour before dawn. Any earlier and he's troubled by insomnia; any later and the encroaching light makes it impossible for him to sleep. He used to enjoy pretending he was a vampire but over the years this has hardened from an affectation to a genuine phobia: if he misses his moment he lies awake, even through that mysterious phase in the circadian cycle when the body's battery is completely drained and the elderly die in hospitals. Ideally, he likes to sleep between four and midday, but often, particularly when he's suffering from jet-lag, which he still suffers from even though as a travel writer he's almost always in an aeroplane, he finds he needs ten hours of rest, so when he awakes in the mid-afternoon it doesn't concern him. He has a vague sense that some internal sensor is warning him that the sun's not where it's supposed to be, but this only distracts Michael for a moment as his eyes focus on the digital clock by his bedside and he realises he has a much larger problem.

He has no idea where he is.

As he gets out of bed he feels such a starburst of head-pain it's as if someone's smashed him with an axe. He lies there for a moment and wills himself to remember. At first he thinks this is just a hangover, but when he touches the back of his head he feels a thick crust of dried blood. The island book, it has to be. He and his two co-writers have such a crazy itinerary for this project that it's not the first time he's forgotten where he is. He remembers flying to Dubrovnik, but there've been so many flights recently. Was that the last? He has memories of an endless boat journey. Ten hours? Twenty? He remembers falling asleep and waking and falling asleep again. For a travel writer Michael has always had a very shaky grasp of geography. He's always far more interested in the destination than the journey. Michael's the only one of the three who can't sail and this makes him dependent on the others during these journeys. Maybe Doug and Carl have played a trick on him. It wouldn't be the first time: once they'd taken him to islands they claimed were Pala and Ernest Legouve Reef only to laugh at him when he filed chapters on those famously fictional locations. Even with their sick Scottish sense of humour, surely they'd draw the line at causing him physical pain? So what had happened? If they'd been set upon by pirates they wouldn't have brought him here afterwards, wherever *here* was. Had he been rescued then? And if so, who by?

He tries standing again. As he does so, he notices a strange flicker in the corner of his vision. It looks like the small blobs that appear on the upper right of a cinema screen that alert the projectionist it's time to change the reel. Before he became a writer Michael's first job was as a film critic. Once he'd noticed these tail leader blobs he'd never been able to ignore them. In those days he'd rarely worn a watch and would work out how much of the film was left by noting the running time, working out how many reels there might be and watching out for the blobs. Most of the time he felt pleased to see them, but there were occasions when he was enjoying a film so much he dreaded the blobs, aware that he was getting closer and closer to real life. It was the same way he felt when he knew he could only snatch a few hours sleep before an early departure. He feels that same dread now.

It's a strange jolt, this next transition. Different from his amnesia before because now he senses something important has happened to him between this reel and the last, although he cannot quite recall what. He's less disconcerted than he was at the start of reel two, prepared now to embrace whatever's happened to his brain to make him see existence in this new way. He also believes he's gained some new skill or knowledge in the elision, but whatever this is, it doesn't, as yet, help him identify his surroundings. He's on a beach, naked apart from his swimming trunks. The beach offers only one immediate clue: in spite of the heat it is largely deserted. He discerns from this that he must be on an unknown or scarcely populated island. Not privately owned: the few people in the sea are not the idle rich. He leans back and enjoys the sun for a moment, before turning on his side and noticing a woman in a blue and scarlet bikini sitting next to a fully dressed older woman. He can tell they are mother and daughter, even though they look nothing alike. The older woman is small and stares at the sea intently; her daughter is rangy and has an innocent, spacey expression.

Before Michael even has the chance to register he is attracted to the younger woman, he finds himself standing up and walking through the hot sand towards her. He feels his mouth open and starts speaking in a language he doesn't know, but hears as English. Michael has always been a terrible monoglot, and realises now that the acquisition of the island's language is his new skill.

"My name is Michael Chambers," he hears himself tell the woman, "I have been coming to this beach every day for the last three weeks. Every day I have looked at you and wanted to come over and introduce myself. I think you are the most beautiful woman I have ever seen and I would love to have the opportunity to get to know you better. If you find this a repulsive idea, or if you already have a husband or a boyfriend, tell me and I will never trouble you again."

Michael stares at the woman. She is shielding her eyes from

the sun and he has no idea whether she has been flattered or insulted by his words. Before she has chance to answer he sees a blur in the corner of his vision. At first he thinks it is just the sun reflected from the sand, but then he realises it's the tail leader blobs again. These reels are so goddamn short; he doesn't understand, why aren't they long enough for him to work out what's happening to him? But it's too late.

Another blob, then another, and that's it: the end of the reel.

Reel 4

When this next reel begins, Michael is aware that he has gone backwards; that his memory is filling in a blank. He is still on the island, now in a queue for an open-air cinema. There are many people in front of him and a few behind. He has come here alone. A man in a red waistcoat with a curled white moustache emerges from the cinema doorway and announces something. Michael doesn't understand the words – he has yet to acquire his ability to decipher the island's language – but assumes he is announcing the start of the show. As he thinks the word 'decipher' it triggers some memory and he reaches into the back pocket of his jeans where he finds a small white notepad. He flicks through it and sees several pages of basic vocabulary, written in his own hand. He reaches into his front pocket and finds a key and a money-clip with a small wad of notes. He takes out a note and squints at it: he may not be much good with languages but knows the currency of almost every country and these notes are like nothing he's ever seen before. Instead of a monarch or historical leader, the notes are decorated with pictures of different animals, like children's money. There is no writing on the notes, just a number to indicate the denomination. He puts the notes back in his pocket and inches forward in the queue.

As he gets closer to the entrance, he passes a poster advertising the night's film. The title of the film is in a script he can't decipher, but he recognises the actor: Al Pacino. Although he has rarely gone to the cinema since quitting as a critic, he always reads reviews and knows the latest film appearances of all the big actors. He has never been a Pacino fan, and the actor has made so many forgettable films in his later career that it's perfectly possible that this is a recent movie he hasn't heard about, but Michael doesn't think that's true. He thinks this is a film that doesn't exist, at least in the world where he used to live.

He reaches the cinema's entrance and watches how much money the person in front of him hands over, taking the same notes from his pocket. He pays for his ticket and finds a seat in the back of the cinema. It takes another ten minutes before the cinema is full and the film begins. There are no trailers and, more unusually, no credits. But there are subtitles. In English. He takes out his notebook and has a sense memory: this is what he has been doing every night for a week, sitting here and trying to work out phonetically words in this new language.

The film has no narrative, and he realises this is not an avant garde film but something stranger. Al Pacino is the only recognisable actor in the movie. The people he talks to all look vaguely familiar, but Michael can't work out where from. Is it possible they might be people he knows? Or used to know? He's not sure. That doesn't seem quite right either.

It is not until he's been watching the film for an hour that he realises this reel is much longer than all the others. And he begins to wonder about his own predicament again. He can't be a character in a film. Even the most eccentric movie wouldn't have a film-within-a-film this long. No this isn't a fictional construction; it is real life. Something has happened to him, that's all, something that's destroyed his perception. Maybe it was the fall from the boat. He is also convinced that this is not a dream. He is not in a coma, he knows that too. Everything feels too real for that. He is on some strange island and for some reason his mind does not want him to know why, or to leave.

Is he dead? No. This is not what death feels like.

Two hours later the film comes to an end. He files out of the open air cinema with the rest of the audience and follows the crowds as they go to cafes for ice cream and beer. He wonders if this reel will last until he meets the woman from the beach again. Maybe this isn't a reel at all. He enters a bar and orders himself a dark beer. Nothing here has a recognisable name and he has to point to every word. But he is satisfied when he gets his drink and goes to sit among strangers in the outside courtyard.

He drinks his beer slowly and is about to get up and return home – he knows where to go and that he is still in the same apartment he woke up in at the beginning of reel two – when the blobs reappear. He is not frightened this time. If he goes backwards, it will solve the questions he wants answered. If he goes forward, then with any luck he will end up in the arms of the girl from the beach. OK, he thinks, bring it on…

Reel 12

Michael is sitting at a table in a small kitchen with four people. Among them is the woman he propositioned on the beach; her mother; a man he immediately realises is her father and a girl in her early teens. They are in the middle of an evening meal and he has a plate of fish, onions and potatoes in front of him. He has a large glass of the same dark beer he drank in the last reel and is holding a small slice of bread. He puts the bread in his mouth and slowly chews it as he listens to the conversation around him. The teenage girl is talking about what she did in class that day. Her family are gently teasing her. He under-stands that he is still on the island and is surprised to hear there is a school here. He suddenly worries about how much time has passed between this reel and the last; how much action he has missed.

"Eva," he says to the woman from the beach, "would you come outside with me for a moment?"

She laughs. "Outside where?"

"Outside," he repeats, and gets up.

He walks to the kitchen's only door and goes outside. It is very dark. Eva follows Michael and puts her arms around him.

"What's wrong?" she asks. "Is it happening again?"

"How long is it since I first came to the island?"

"I don't know. I can tell you how long it is since you met me."

"OK."

"Six years."

"Six years?" he repeats.

"Yes," she says. "You haven't forgotten, have you?"

"No, not at all. It's just, I feel afraid…"

"Of the dots."

"What?"

"The dots, the blobs, whatever they are. The things you scream about in your sleep."

"Have I seen them before?"

"Yes. Twice."

"When? How long ago?"

"I don't remember. Honestly, you mustn't worry; nothing is going to take you away from me."

"How can you be so sure?"

"I'm sure, Michael. Kiss me."

He does so. He is about to follow her back inside when he feels a moment of pure fear and then there they are. It starts with a flicker and then no amount of blinking can obscure them: the tail leader blobs, back one last time, he realises. There is nothing that's going to come after this, no way he can be saved. He knows he's not going to go backwards, whoever has strung together this life for him has nothing more to offer: the missing moments of his life on the island are gone forever, as is, he fears, everything he experienced before coming here.

There's no getting around it.

Goodbye Michael.

It's the end of the final reel.

5-4-3-2-1 FINISH.

THE SAND EATERS

GINNY BAILY

> Ask them why they idle there
> While we suffer, and eat sand,
> And the crow and the vulture
> Hover always above our broken fences
> And strangers walk over our portion.
> ('Songs of Sorrow', Kofi Awoonor)

The old woman was folded into the base of the tree, her back propped against the trunk. Her patterned blue wrap was rucked up around bony knees and her flint-thin shins stretched out into the sunlight. Her bare black feet, baking in the sulphurous heat, flopped outward at a careless angle. A pair of green flip-flops was placed neatly alongside. From the knees up she was obscured by the shadow cast by the tree's branches as if she'd been planted and had taken on the characteristics of an extra knobbly root, quiet and deep in the narrow shade of the high afternoon sun. She sat unmoving, seeming to gaze through a gap between the huts that encircled this central space. She stared past her own hut and her neighbour's, Old Man Sebo's, to the empty track beyond.

At her back, behind and around the houses of the little village scratched out of the bush, stood the great, dank expanse of rainforest. It covered the uplands and reached over the borders into the countries beyond.

In front, eddies of a wind that had travelled from the Sahara, thickened with flakes of charred thatch, played with the sandy soil, lifting it into ridges and flattening them again. Gusts billowed Old Man Sebo's jacket, which hung from a nail on the back of his flung-open door. They puffed up the sleeves, animating them into weakly flailing arms. The jacket was now so threadbare and filthy that its original colour had dulled to the sludge brown of dead leaves after the rain, but Old Man Sebo had cut a dash when he wore it. He completed his daily outfit with a yellow cane and a pink brimless hat worn low on his brow. At night he always hung the jacket on the door-hook, smoothing its creases with a respectful motion of his hand. He'd never let it be cleaned because it was only the weave of age-old dirt that held it together. The hot wind that wore it now didn't show the same restraint.

The rice kitchen was still smouldering after three days. The torched huts had gone up like kindling, but the tightly packed sacks of grain held the fire in a slow pungent burn. The aroma of slow-cooking rice wafted through the village like a profligate feast, the event of such importance that the whole harvest had been donated, with no thought of tomorrow. Both the rain-fed upland rice and the swamp rice the villagers cultivated, which they had sown, picked, dried and stored and was to last the whole season, all blown in one blaze. The old lady was known for her Jollof rice, which she served with hot pepper sauce, fried plantains, green bananas and collard greens or sweet potato leaves. On this occasion, she didn't stir from her place beneath the tree.

The people who'd swarmed through the village hadn't wanted the rice. They'd taken only what was easy and wouldn't slow them, what could be carried without breaking their stride: the dried meat, eddoes, cassava and palm nuts. They'd taken the cane juice to drink later around their camp fire but left the sacks of rice; their futures so assured they had no need of supplies. Their life was only then, in that dazzling blade of a moment.

Brightly coloured items of clothing were scattered about the dusty pathways of the village like fallen bunting, caught on fences or half trampled into the earth: women's wraps in bold patterns of yellow and emerald green; a red t-shirt and a torn blue one; a child's plastic sandal, its strap broken; two bobble hats with dirty yellow rims; a strip of cloth in bright turquoise that might have served as a scarf, belt or bandanna. Another wad of cloth, a faded pink coil used for balancing a load upon the head, was wedged between an overturned pink and yellow-striped bowl and a kettle. In front of the largest house, the only one to have a tin roof and a verandah, lay a battered brown suitcase. Its contents spilled onto the earth between two spiky clumps of elephant grass. Strewn like diamonds among the enamel cups and plates, a crimson blanket and a tub of palm butter, were broken pieces of mirror. They caught the sunlight and shimmered it up into the air or held it in sparkling little pools of concentrated light.

The mirror used to hang on the wall opposite the doorway, showing the comings and goings of the family and their visitors. Often it held the daughter's face, her lips, the curve of her cheek and the braids in her hair. When the shout came to run for your life, the soldiers were coming, people scooped up their children and ran. Some snatched up food, blankets, clothes and cups. There was no time to pack. The brown suitcase must have been for a different, scheduled journey. The girl, spinning round in the house to find her most precious possession, saw the mirror, pulled it from the wall and ran, clutching it to her chest. Sometimes the mirror had held a child spinning his hoop through the door and grinning at his sister's sly looking-glass expression. Today, it held only sky.

The emptied village was filling with grit and sand like a bottle cast up by the tide. The hot wind seemed to draw a whistle from its lips, the high, keening sound of the emptiness.

Not all the villagers had run. The old, the slow and the sleepy were left behind. The sun had shifted and now the old lady was almost entirely exposed to its blistering heat as she had been the day before and the day before that. She sat unmoving, not even brushing sand from her eyes. She was used to extremes. It would have been cooler in the dark corners of her little house on the other side of the clearing. The bamboo window was propped open. Through it came a slant-ing shaft of golden light flecked with sparks of dust and sooty embers. A yellow gourd filled with palm wine gleamed on the sunlit table. Flies landed on the white tin plate and scaled the remains of a mound of rice, treading it down, palpating and reshaping its contours with their spindly black legs. Ants and beetles and other winged insects came creeping and scuttling and whirring across the dusty floor or through the hazy air. The old lady's broom and a shovel lay beside her as though she'd thought to sweep away the debris and the unseemly mess but had sat down to take stock before beginning. Inside her house, the insects' scratchings and swishings and buzzings ventilated the silence as they found their way into unswept corners and under the bed where the old lady herself had dutifully lain, three days earlier.

'Get under the bed,' her husband told her, 'I'll be back in a minute.' He believed in respect for the elders and the power of parley. He stood at their threshold and waited. From her squeezed and breathless hiding place she could see only his trousered legs and sandalled feet, planted firmly in their open doorway. There was the clamour of a wild party outside. Music with a beat as fast as her heart blasted from somewhere nearby and voices joined in, not singing but chanting. Men shouted, ordering the remaining people out of their houses, demanding to know what tribe they were. The doorway lightened momentarily as the old woman's husband moved back inside. He resumed his position but now the knife for cutting into the rubber trees swung from his right hand. The shouting and yelling continued and someone burst into laughter, a wheezing cackle of a laugh, that suddenly stopped.

An unknown child appeared in the clearing, dancing in front of her husband and singing a strange song in his high, fluting voice. He jumped from foot to foot, swirling something that glittered silver in front of him. Then there were screams and the crackling of flames, the sweet smell of thatch like burning stubble, the poisonous fumes of plastic, a sickening stench of singed animal hair and seared flesh, like bush meat. Booted feet crowded her husband and he disappeared. There were gunshots just outside the window and a grunt that sounded like a pig, although they didn't keep one.

The soldiers dragged Old Man Sebo out into the yard. As the old woman watched them roll him inside his own mattress, tie him up with string like fufu wrapped in plantain leaves and put a match to the parcel they'd made, she thought of her children and her grandchildren. Smoke rose in a bluish plume and she willed their feet into a blur of speed.

Later, when most of the fires had died down and the old lady had taken up her place beneath the tree, the vultures came. After them came the monkeys. It started with one monkey, scattering husks from the branches above, and then dropping down to the ground in a rustle of leaves. It landed near the old woman's feet, batted at her flip flops, and as if disturbed by her indifference, danced backwards with its tail raised. It paused at the open doorway of Old Man Sebo's house and yowled, a piercing shriek which summoned a horde of other monkeys down from the trees. Suddenly, there were monkeys everywhere, darting in and out of the burnt-out huts, squawking from the ruined roofs. For a brief time, the village belonged to them. Then came a boom, a distant sound that might have been the thunder announcing rain at last, or might have been gunfire. The monkeys ran back into the forest and left the village empty again.

The hush that wrapped the empty village now held no human sound, but wove into itself the squawks of the monkeys, the swooping cries of birds, the buzz and hum of insects, the creak of branches.

The sun had sunk low. It balanced on the tree line, casting its last light on the village before it dipped away. The village seemed less a man-made thing than an organism thrown up by the earth itself. In the light that filtered through the treetops, the earth, with its buried and unburied bones, its matted roots and trampled fence posts, glowed red.

PRESSED FLOWER

ADAM THORPE

Something made him recoil from all mention of her. It was not the circumstances, it was this other thing, this element of strangeness and even terror, the kind of terror a large owl's wingbeat brings as it thuds slowly through a midnight wood. Elfin spirits, eyes in the darkness, goblins in the bole of a tree.

Ever since the hanging he had been like this. He did not even know the details. He did not wish to know the details.

"Do you ever want to go out there, Mike, see where it happened?"

No, he did not. He didn't even know where it had happened. A factory precinct, probably.

Mike sat behind an opening carved out of the books stacked from wall to ceiling, cataloguing on the computer, reading, thinking. The opening was about the size of a large telly, as his friend Alex observed. Alex was a living Lincoln legend – the classics graduate who owned the second-hand electrical goods store up the lane: people flocked. "Reminds me of watching the test card when I was a kid."

"Exciting childhood, you must have had, Alex."

"Oh. Have I never told you about it?"

The trouble with friends and the more regular customers was that their jokes came round again and again. The radio, soughing in dismay when it wasn't on 98.3 Herz., trickled along in company, rarely playing the Beethoven he preferred. Hour by hour, day by day, he felt he was growing fatter and balder and uglier. "Not possible," Alex would reassure him. "There are limits. Even the universe has limits."

Sarah's volume of poems was on display in the window, at full price. It was out of kilter with the rest, his stock's cream: the morocco-bound, signed Kipling with only slight foxing; the early Akhmatova in Russian with loose boards, otherwise a very fresh copy; the 1864 guide to Lincoln Cathedral, slightly shaken, a few marginal markings; the rare edition of Wilkie Collins's *Basil*, one page badly browned by a pressed flower.

Against these her homespun cover screeched in Post-it yellow, an indestructible chemical in fine soil. He despised the terrible title, *Now We Are Speaking As One*. He pretended to others that he felt obliged to carry it, to do what he could in her memory; he could hardly tell them the truth.

The clippings graced the pin-board like old blooms on a grave, illuminated by a shaft of sunlight for about twenty minutes on clear days. The paper was tanning at the edges; the colour photos in the *Guardian* article were not so much fading as fogging up. He looked alarmingly younger; she remained what she always was.

"Time to take this lot down, Mike?" suggested Alex, one morning. "In the name of preservation?"

"Preservation of what? Me?"

"In pickle. *Homo obsoletus*."

He recalled, again and again, the first time he'd come across her book, on a chilly February afternoon some eight years before.

Whenever it was dry, he would take out an old pinewood box of £1 bargains, desperate stuff, and place it on a fold-out table to the left of the door. Designed to lure the fish inside the shop's net, the titles remained stubbornly unsold; they'd take on a sad, warped look until his periodic clean-outs.

Because he knew the box's contents by heart (their arrangement like a view of familiar hills), he immediately noticed the new addition at closing time. It had been slipped between a third edition of James Elroy Flecker's *Hassan*, broken spine repaired with gaffer tape, and a horribly authentic 1970s hardback, *The Future of Nuclear Deterrence*.

Despite its garishness, the volume was a proper slim hardback. He didn't recognise the publisher, Agitation Press. Its poems on the unfortunate paper (much too white, slippery to the touch) were very poor: a whisker away from greetings-card verse only by dint of their political content. The English was not as perfect as the author probably believed. In place of the latter's name were three initials: S H T. Like a command to be quiet and listen.

He left the book where it had been inserted, intrigued rather than irritated. One day, he was sure, its progenitor would come by, for he was in no doubt that the poet herself (the gender being evident in several of the poems, as well as the probability of her Chinese origins) was responsible for this original type of distribution.

It was amusing, and then irritating, to find the book repeatedly placed, front jacket up, on top of the others, too squarely to be the action of a careless customer. He failed to catch the culprit. She must, he thought, wait for him to disappear into the basement in search of some recondite request, or sense him vanishing into the labyrinth of his on-screen catalogue, before pouncing.

He installed a tinkly bell on the door, like an old-fashioned grocer's. It made no difference: the displacement would happen every month or so over a two-year period, and he began to suspect that it was a peculiar game rather than the furtive manipulation of stock that even reputable authors indulged in. Again and again he pretended to descend into the basement, returning abruptly and startling the customer whose guilt he had wrongly suspected.

He even suspected Alex, and – like a boy detective – scattered flour on the book's cover.

"What are you looking at my privates for, Mike?"

"I'm looking at your hands. Show me your hands."

"From off your stock, friend." It was dust. Very unprofessional.

He even imagined, at times, that he had just spotted a shadow passing across the many panes of the bay window, and would hurtle outside (in his ungainly fashion) and glance up and down the quiet lane, wheezing away, only to notice the book in its customary position, like a shout amidst murmurs.

He left a clashing mauve Post-it on the cover: *I know who you are*. It was still stuck on there when he discovered the book propped on the window sill a fortnight later. *And I know you!* had been added, in a clumsy scrawl. He felt manipulated, and resented it. He began to anticipate the interference; it made him nervous. But he wasn't a surveillance camera, although Alex offered an antique black-and-white model from 1984 for a fiver: "Makes everyone look like a phantom."

"Then what does it make real phantoms look like?"

"Oh, you'd just come out invisible, Mike."

He only came across her in the flesh because Alex dragged him along to a poetry reading in the town hall – an event in aid of Amnesty to which too many local bards had gained permission to contribute. After two hours, numbed by the fervent versifying, he was about to slip away for a pint when a small, slim woman in a bright red dress mounted the stage, identified herself with a clear laugh as Tibetan-Chinese-*Irish*, and began to deliver – in a high monotone – lines that rang familiarly in Mike's ears. The book she was holding was a book he knew so well that he felt she had stolen it from him.

The audience clapped her enthusiastically, relieved to have an authentic victim after a run of local wannabes whose main claim to political suffering was not being taken seriously in the pub. She wore black-rimmed glasses and had a homely, run-of-the-mill appearance; her favourite poet was Keats. Mike was disappointed. He had no recollection of ever having seen her before. Her name was Sara.

He noted where she was sitting and followed her out into the main street at the end of the show. She gave another clear laugh when he was introduced by a mutual acquaintance – a flamboyant, vaguely-punk performance poet in his late thirties called Murray Drill who would bore Mike stiff in the shop every few months with tales of bogus derring-do from his London days.

"I know you," she chirruped, removing her glasses and revealing chestnut-coloured eyes.

"And I know you," Mike quoted, attempting to sound conspiratorial.

"Murray's told me everything on *you*," she insisted.

"Everything?"

"You're *very* expert in old books."

Murray chortled and Alex coughed. Mike ignored them. "Not all my stock is old. Yours isn't, for instance. It keeps popping up."

"Oh, that's nice," she smiled, with a shy look. Mike felt his heart swell; he'd forgotten his heart was even there and this swelling was a surprise, like an old leathery balloon becoming smooth and beautiful.

"Yeah," he went on, somewhat remorselessly; "in fact I like your poems. I like your absolute belief in them, that they should be *prominent*, sort of *on top*."

"I speak for my people," she said, her face taking on a fierceness that instantaneously banished the homely side. "My poems are my people speaking, in their oppression and their suffering. Since the Chinese invaded my country, they have killed more than one million of my people. All their ghosts are *speaking* through my poems," she added, her eyes flashing, her mouth bracketed by two deep dimples that caught the street light on their flanks and into which Mike felt he was plummeting stereoscopically.

"Come on, honey," said Murray, placing an arm around her tiny waist and giving her a squeeze. "Let's get ourselves home before you take on the Red Army."

"I'm not even a foot soldier," Mike blurted, astonished and dismayed at the idea of Murray being her lover as well as mentor.

And they all laughed: even Alex.

She had a room in one of the duller Lincoln suburbs and he wandered down there one weekend with a nice Everyman *Keats*, but lost his bottle when he saw Murray's motorbike parked in front.

Then the poet did the poetic thing by skidding under a truck, and her own volume stayed put. It had been poor old

Murray all along, of course. Bound to have been. But Mike didn't have the heart to remove it from the box entirely.

Sara popped up one day with Murray's library, mostly obscure rock commemorations with beer-spill on the colour plates. Mike swiftly discovered, after a fumbling, blushing attempt to take her out for a drink, that she was not interested in him as anything but intellectual stimulus. He gave her the Keats anyway, and apologised for the tanning.

"Tanning?"

"It means the paper's gone yellow. Acid in the paper, eating at it. The first step towards complete disintegration. Like me going bald here," he added, pointing to where his topknot once flourished.

"Thank you!" she cried. But he felt he'd blown it for good.

She dropped in almost every week, however, for her bout of intellectual stimulus, the odd purchase. She told him all about the appalling conditions in Chinese factories, "worse than Dickens", and how they "get rid of people who complain".

"Twelve-hour shifts, seven days a week, no sick pay, no rights! To make Barbies! For 70p a day! For you westerners!"

"I promise I won't play with my Barbie ever again," he said.

His heart stayed uninflated, guarded as he was. The Irish bit of her was from her grandfather, a Protestant hydraulics engineer who had fallen for more than the Himalayas in the 1930s. He found her presence as trying, eventually, as any other customer – more so, even; she exposed his own inadequacies, a recognition of his failures with women. She even tried to take photos of him for some protest magazine, on the basis that he was carrying her book. He loathed being photographed or filmed: it shattered the vague illusion (as he once put it after a few pints with Alex and friends) that he was not a freak of nature. "*You're* not a freak of nature, Mike," they all chorused, faux-sympathetically, like nurses.

Being responsible for his senile mother did not help matters, even when she was placed in a home. It was a shock when he discovered that Sara was a geriatric care assistant, working mostly nights, and that this was by her own choice. Their conversations began to revolve, not around poetry, nor even

China, but around the peculiarly fascinating medical details of old age.

The book was firmly displayed in the window, of course, by this stage.

"Still not sold," she sighed.

"Hey, Sara, how did Murray fox me for so long?"

"Fox?"

"You know, fool me? Moving your book around when I wasn't looking? Because I *was* looking."

Her chestnut eyes seemed puzzled, genuinely so, above her smile. He'd read somewhere that the Chinese smiled when they were pained, and he dropped the subject, fairly pained himself. Yes, may Murray rest in peace.

When she announced her intention to return to Tibet for at least a year – clandestinely, if needed – he joked that by the time she got back, her book *might* just be sold.

"If it is not, I shall blame you, Mike," she said, darkly – adding that bright laugh.

That was the last time he saw her. Three – no, *four* years back, now. She did write to him from Tibet. She had discovered the very house of her maternal grandmother (killed during the invasion), and suggested they might both live there "like brother and sister, writing poems and meditating on our meaning of existence." He felt physically ill with dread, reading it that grey day. It was all possible, even at forty-five. As Sarah's title poem put it:

> Hope for every
> thing
> expect no   thing.

He looked up from his cubbyhole. A single customer was smiling through an erotic volume from the seventies that Mike himself would enjoy – entranced by its glossy photographs of couplings under a sun-filled haze of leaflight in a time belonging to his childhood, the haircuts laughable above the dateless flesh. Similarly, Mike felt he was reading a letter from the far past describing a future he had already experienced and which was now over. In other words, he had no choice but to go out and live in the snowbound mountains of Tibet, sowing his terraces and drinking (he supposed) rice wine.

The next day he was humping flimsy boxes over-laden with nice Victorian volumes, mostly bound in gilt-stamped half-calf, job lots from an auction, when the sky cracked open and it bucketed; the two boxes remaining in the back of the van got soaked as a gust drove the rain horizontal while he was struggling across the road.

That was the day (he later calculated) that it happened.

"Hardly very sporting," as Alex commented. There was a brief flurry of interest in the better papers (thus the clippings), a couple of poems published, a short profile in *Index on Censorship*, a full page in the *Lincolnshire Gazette* considerably eaten into by an advert for local car hire, but nothing more. Mike suspected official interference, to do with the Olympic Games: diplomatic nudges in the gloomy, hidden passages under the bland architecture, beneath all that surface celebration of peace and togetherness.

By that time, anyway, her Tibetan project had turned into what sounded very much like dodgy political agitation in central China, stirring up trouble in the 70p-a-day factories and sweatshops; Mike had already been wondering whether Sara would be the same person when she returned. No one could tell him why she had been hanged, or by whom, or even where, only that the deed was done. He ignored the rumour that it was suicide, the martyr's desperate gesture: the only good poem she would ever write.

He made vague approaches to the Chinese authorities – travelling from Lincoln down to London at his own expense – and wrote an article for the *Sunday Times* which was rehashed out of existence by a sub and referred to him as "Sara Hsai-Tung's partner", when he was nothing of the sort. Then the media interest vanished, overnight.

Seated behind his books, the little gas cooker nudging his spine, the Lincolnshire twilight fogging the bay window and tea-coloured mould growing on the ceiling, he found himself glancing up at a shuffle or a squeak, even when there was a customer in the shop; if the place was empty, sweat broke out on his face (he had always thought this an invention of nineteenth-century novelists) and his hand would tremble, adding a trail of noughts to the pencilled price on the flyleaf or making it impossible to type on the laptop.

As a child he had been petrified by a school reading of *The Brown Hand*, and now envisaged Sara's bony knuckles rapping slowly on the wooden panel of his door, loosening his little notices pinned there – *Please Do NOT Park In Front Of The Window. Complete Set Of Dickens Needs To Find Its Loving Owner – Apply Within. Voted Best Second-Hand Bookshop in Lincoln By Those IN THE KNOW* – so that they fluttered to her green feet and she had to step over them as the door swung open of its own accord. All this he imagined as if it was about to happen. He considered seeing somebody professional about it.

It would fade for a few weeks, and he would forget his own fear, the intensity of it. Then without warning it would return. It exhausted him, this release and capture, capture and release. Regulars started to comment on his pallor, asking if he was "all right"; though they rarely were themselves, from the look of it.

He could hardly tell them the truth.

The fact is, Sara's book had started walking again. It had kept moving every few weeks from wherever he had placed it – in the pine box, on the central table, in the poetry shelves – until his decision to display its yellow garishness prominently once more in the window had brought a semblance of calm. A semblance only: within, he was in turmoil.

Then the day came when Alex, so thin in his raincoat that his spectacles stuck out either side of his face, brought up the subject of Sarah after at least two years of her name being absent from Mike's workaday life. Alex was discoursing on the Olympic torch protests, and mentioned Sarah as an example – a rare example – of someone who had "more than just talked". Mike nodded, feeling a sudden dread close about him, an almost physical darkness, as if someone were pulling up the old wooden shutters that he would, some day soon, get round to mending.

Alex had a partiality for sherbert fountains, and would hand one over to Mike most times he popped in: a gauche echo of boyhood. Instantaneously convinced that Sarah's ashes were somehow mixed up in the sherbert powder he was sampling, Mike scuttled downstairs, washing out his mouth in the basement's tiny loo. "I am the victim of a saddo's delusion," he muttered to himself. "Nevertheless, I have just tasted her ashes on my tongue. They are fizzing and eating into my tongue." He saw in his mind the page of the Wilkie Collins browned by the pressed flower: his own heart, ruined.

He stayed in the loo until he heard Alex, who wasn't the type to be bothered by such rudeness, leave the shop. Then Mike crept out and stood trembling by the main table, leaning on it, finding a space for his hands between the smart coffee-table volumes now relegated to a strange and ignominious afterlife, a purgatory of perpetual shuffling from box to box, their bright colours faded by shafts of sunlight in unknown rooms – embodiments of hope's failure, of expectation's duty to be quiet, of all that withering business.

He went over to the window display and removed Sarah's book and carried it down to the basement, sliding it under a heavy, six-volume set of Carlyle's essays, long webbed by deceased spiders. Buried by history, he thought to himself, with a kind of wry astonishment at his own sang-froid, his perverse courage.

Whereupon he heard a creak from the floorboards above, and then another, although the tinkle of the door's bell had never sounded.

He knew, as he stood there trembling in the one-bulb basement murk, that she would have a smile on her lips; that she would look the very embodiment of health. As if (he thought to himself with his own surprised wheeze of laughter) the city had yielded an unknown saint from its cathedral tomb, and the long centuries had left no stains on the white skin.

IN TRANSIT

FRANCES MERIVALE

I'm stuck to the leather seat of a taxi, my thigh sweating against a stranger's. This is how it goes. It's midnight and Dubai is a sauna. The driver's door is open but not a flicker of air comes through it. Outside is as hot as inside and only the stars look cold.

Six of us are rammed in, four women in the back and two men squashed into the passenger seat, waiting to be taken to the transit hotel. On my left are two middle-aged women in safari shorts, varicose veins swelling up in the heat, on my right a young student with short hair and a pierced lip. The younger man in front glances back at us, his facial hair finely crafted and his shirt a plastic shade of red. The old man next to him is bald and glistening. Every few seconds he wipes his head with a handkerchief. After a while he stops wiping it and says, "We are not sardines."

No one else has said a word. It's late and we're all on different time zones. Mine is Greenwich Meantime, a scratchy 8pm. Adrian will have called by now. He'll wonder why my desk was empty.

My ticket is for Comoros. This is hardly the direct route but I've learnt you can fly anywhere cheap as long as it's via Dubai. I've done this before. Only this time I didn't bring any luggage. Nor did I book the hotel.

"We," says the old man again, "are not sardines."

The girl next to me sniggers and one of the women lets out a hot sigh. I try not to move. It will only draw attention to the sweat between us. Instead I fix on the drips forming like pus on the old man's scalp.

"We are *not* sardines."

This time the guy with the goatee shifts over and hangs one arm out of the window, only it looks limp so he brings it in again and hooks it on the doorframe. Poser. I stare out at the runway.

Finally the driver appears. He pastes himself into the seat and starts the engine. It sets a cassette running, something that sounds like Madonna being strangled in fast-forward. We drive out of the airport towards the dregs of the city that circuit the terminal like under-brewed tea. Dust flies in and cakes the sweat to my skin. I half close my eyes. An image of Adrian hits me: of the surprise on his face when he realised where I was touching him. "I don't normally do this," he said. I told him, "I do." Afterwards he said I was a beautiful person. I said, "You don't know me," and picked up his inflatable globe.

The hotel is a large, glossy affair with mirrors on every wall and reception staff dressed in sequined suits. The varicose veins have gone up to their room and so has the student. The old man is pacing the lobby, raising his arms and glorifying the air-conditioning to heaven. Which leaves the guy with the goatee and me at the desk.

"I'm afraid we're fully booked," says the receptionist. Her lips sparkle like the sequins.

I look at the chairs in the corner of the lobby. "My flight's at nine," I say. "Couldn't I just crash here till then?"

Her lipstick un-sticks and the smile falls. "I'm sorry."

Without meaning to, I catch Goatee's eyes. "Are you stuck too?" I ask him.

He clears his throat. "Actually I have a room booked." He hands his card to the receptionist. "The name's Toole," he says.

She clocks him in and hands him a key card.

"Hey, the bar's twenty-four hours," Toole says to me, "You could always wait there." He sounds American.

I glance at the bar and then back at the receptionist. She purses her lips.

"I'll be paying for drinks," I say. I give her an innocent, slightly needy smile, one I usually use on men. Toole catches it and smiles back.

"How about I keep you company?" He says it as if he's doing me a favour but he's looking at my cleavage. I try not to focus on the beard.

There's a brief wait while someone comes to take his bag, then we head to the bar.

"So what's your first name, Toole?"

"Dan," he says.

We take a seat on embroidered cushions laid out like airport souvenirs. There are no other customers. "I'm Carrie," I say.

He nods at my chest. In the heat I've undone one button too far.

A barman comes over and asks what we'd like. Dan asks for a beer and I say I'll take the same. When it comes, he gulps from the bottle and makes a noise about it. "I sure needed that," he says, "Geeze, was that sardine guy weird?"

I laugh. Men like it when you laugh at what they say.

"So where are you headed?" he asks.

"Comoros."

"Yeah?" He hasn't a clue. "I'm going to Bangkok."

"Great," I say.

He looks pleased and adjusts himself on the cushion. "I'm trying not to have too many expectations," he says. "You know, Thailand… sex, drugs, ladyboys… I'm not going for all that. I'm going for myself. My girlfriend's been getting heavy, you know. I think I just need some space – to figure out who *I* am again."

He's one of those. Every trip I meet at least one who offloads his entire life story in five minutes. I pour beer into my glass and watch the bubbles rise. The lights make them sparkle. The whole bar is reflected four times over in the mirrors, creating the blurred effect of a glitzy church. My mother would be horrified.

"So I guess I picked Bangkok because there's no way Susie would ever go there. She's kinda conservative. Maybe I need to get it out of my system…"

"Maybe you need to get it into your system," I say, calling the barman over for another beer. I didn't mean much by it but Dan is giving it intense consideration, nodding and screwing up his forehead. He's probably in therapy.

"You're right, you know. God, I think you're onto something. I mean, all my life I've done the right thing. I got the grades, went to med school, met a girl... What I need to do is go crazy."

I glaze over and my mind drifts back to Adrian. Last night was crazy for him. He'll be in the room where we were and it will seem empty now, though it's been empty most nights. He'll pick up the inflatable globe and wonder...

I told him once how sometimes I like to disappear. He looked confused. He's the only one in the office still oblivious to my exploits – to the fact that I've had sex with almost every male on the fourth floor, even Alf from I.T. He thinks I'm just friendly. I'm friendly to him even though the others aren't. He buys me sandwiches when I'm too busy to stop for lunch – and if he goes to Sainsburys he buys me *Taste the Difference* ones and says, "You know what, you really can." These are the things I know about him. At some point soon he will call me because he's not the type to have a one-night stand. He thinks this is the start of something.

"Are you listening Carrie?"

"Huh?"

We're on our third beer and Dan's still talking.

"Well you seem easy-going, you know, liberal-minded. Sure you know what it's like when you just need a break."

"Yes," I say, looking at him properly for the first time, "I do."

Sometimes that's all it takes – a brief connection. When it happens I can ignore the fact that his facial hair is sculpted like a suburban hedge, that he has those small, sincere eyes that never really look at me, that he's rested a hand on the inside of his thigh as if to draw my attention there, that he's so self-absorbed he'd miss a cyclone.

He checks his watch. "Wow, we've been talking a long time."

I nod.

"Listen, my room's a double. You're welcome to... you know." I think he winks but it's hard to tell when I've drunk a bit and his eyes are so small. Then I see his hand move closer to his crotch.

"I'm pretty tired," I say.

He swallows the last of his beer and eyes the door. "Come on."

It's a king size bed. I lie on my back in my white shirt and knickers. Dan has his boxers on. He hitches the sheet down to his hips so I can see his chest heaving up and down. It's a chest he's dedicated as much time to as the goatee. He puts his hands behind his head, revealing neat tufts of underarm hair. His nipples are hard as screws.

"This is what I love," he says, "This kind of random thing that can happen on the road."

"You call this the road?"

"Well, you know... life." He turns his head to look at me.

"We're in transit," I say. I turn to the wall. Then I feel it. The hand. First it touches my side, then gets under my shirt and creeps up towards my armpit and over to my breast. I don't move. Some people take that as a sign of consent. I hear the bed creak before I feel the next move. Then suddenly he's over me, a dense mass of sculpted muscle easing down level as an ironing board, his skin shiny and firm.

"Carrie?" he says, searching for a reaction.

Mechanically, I run a hand down his back towards his arse and he bucks forward and presses between my legs. I get a hand beneath him and nudge at his hip.

"You have a girlfriend," I say.

"Not like you." He kisses my neck.

"What am I?" I hadn't meant to say it out loud.

"Hot," he says.

When I was a teenager I did it to spite my mother. The day she realised I'd humped half the boys at The Holy Ghost of St. Stephen she turned electric blue and said the devil had made

100

me. She used to crawl up the walls with that stuff. Now the anger has turned to disappointment and she's shut herself up indoors. "I don't want to go out," she tells me. "Not if this is what the world has made of you."

I want to tell her, "I made me," I want to tell her, "You made me." Sometimes I think it would make her sick. Other times I think she might cry and hold on to me. I'm not ready for either, so for now I keep still.

It doesn't take Dan long and then he rolls off me and falls asleep. Soon after that he starts snoring. I hold my watch up to the window and check the time. Another three hours before I have to go; I could still get some sleep.

I get up and slide past Dan off the end of the bed. In one of the cupboards I find blankets and arrange them in a pile on the floor with a pillow. The snoring is getting violent. I get up again, pull on my clothes and take the bedding out to the corridor and arrange it close to the wall so I'm out of the way. It's quiet here and I'm alone. It makes my skin feel dirty.

When you've done it as much as I have, you start to wonder where the boundary is. Who wouldn't I let have me? I did it with Alf from I.T. and that slimy motorbike salesman, why not this freak as well? Make a collection of them; I'm going to hell anyway, I may as well take a scrapbook. But every time they pull out, a piece of me goes with them. They fall asleep and spit it out. There are islands of me spat out around the world now. One day I'll go to them.

This is how it happened with Adrian. I was stressed over the sales figures and he asked if I wanted to go for a drink. Just us. He was sweet about it and we sat in a booth and talked about our families. He said his were worried he didn't get out enough. I said mine thought I got out too much. It didn't occur to me until he turned red and asked if I'd like another drink that he considered this a date. I tried not to laugh and said, 'How about we get something to eat?" His face fell when he explained he had to get back to feed his sister's cat. I said, "I'll come with you. We can get takeaway." Then there was the problem of his bicycle. He didn't want to leave it, but he was worried it'd be rude to let me travel separately. I said he should go wild, leave the bike and cycle back tomorrow instead. Eventually he agreed. I grabbed his helmet. He put on his reflective jacket and we took the train.

There's a place I go in my head called 'in transit'. It's an airport lounge with rows and rows of plastic yellow chairs screwed down to the floor. I sit on one of them cross-legged and focus on the reflection of myself in the window and try very hard to feel what's left of my own skin. If I don't move, I might be able to.

I don't know why I made the move on Adrian. Maybe it was somewhere to be last night. Maybe it was because when I sat there on his living room floor singing along to *God Gave Rock n' Roll To You*, I knew he was looking at me. It wasn't the way others look at me. He was looking at me as if I were someone amazing.

At last I'm dozing in the hotel corridor but the peace is broken by the sound of someone muttering and pacing towards me. He draws closer and trips on my foot.

"Good gracious, a beggar."

It's old man sardines and he's still in his clothes.

"Sorry," I say, sitting up.

He stares at me. "Are you a prostitute?" he says.

"No."

"You look like a prostitute. I knew one once."

"Thanks." I rub my eyes.

"Her name was Helena."

"Mine's Carrie," I say.

He goes on looking at me, and then gestures the length of the corridor. "I was just walking the plains."

"I'm sorry I got in the way." I stand up and check the time. "I have to get a flight soon anyway."

"Is that your room?"

"I don't have a room."

"Come to mine. It's romantic."

I laugh. "Not if you think I'm a prostitute."

"You're not a prostitute. Who ever said that?"

I shrug. He pads back down the corridor and I let the blankets go but keep hold of the pillow.

"So where are you going to?" I ask him after I've followed him up three flights of stairs.

"Room 443."

"I meant after that."

"Oh. This is it for me."

He doesn't switch the light on. For a moment I freeze in the doorway, the pillow clutched to my middle. I don't want anyone else tonight. But the old man smiles and beckons me in. I take a step forward and peer round to see that the entire far wall is a window looking out over Dubai. The city is split into islands of light and behind them is the desert.

"Have a seat." He gestures to the bed. I hesitate before going in and he stands there tapping his leg.

"Splendid, isn't it?" He sweeps his arm towards the window.

I sit down and look out. Dawn is approaching and the sky is an unclean orange over temples and skyscrapers and forgotten flat roofs.

The old man gets out his handkerchief. "Makes me hot just to look at it," he says, mopping his forehead.

I hug my arms around my chest and try not to look at him. But he fixes on me as if I'm a tropical insect.

"Did you know they eat salad for breakfast in this country?" he says.

I nod and rub at the dry skin on my elbows.

"Real live lettuce leaves and tomato and... cucumber."

"I've been here before," I tell him.

"Have you really? What an adventurer."

I stare past him at the view, the familiar early morning smear from another man's window.

"I've been around," I say.

At this, he takes his eyes off me and turns back to the window. The sun has risen above the horizon and you can see the dust thickening outside. I sit very still and try to think of all the places I haven't been touched: under my fingernails, the sides of my knees, my wrists, the tops of my ears, that dent where my scalp meets the back of my neck. There's more than I thought.

CARIBBEAN HONEYMOON

KEITH JARDIM

It is a hot, late afternoon and the young woman and man are being driven through the city, near the sea, past the financial district. The squat concrete buildings – banks, lawyers' offices, and insurance companies – shade the car intermittently, but offer no relief from the heat. The car, rattling like a rusty tambourine, soon passes former colonial homes with high ceilings and pointed roofs, many of them now quaint restaurants with large windows. Their newly painted interiors, peach and lime-green cool, are crowded with customers. Waiters move quickly about, serving the executives and lawyers clusters of ice-cold bottled beer.

The sea and sky are now a grey mass, and the dust and haze from the mountains in the north continue to drift into the city, into the car. They are moving through hotter air, in the oldest part of the city now. Motorists shout and blow their horns at the bullying tactics of their driver; luxury cars career out of his way. They pass statues of political-leaders and calypsonians of dark bronze, the leaders with indifferent gazes – dull faces, blank eyes that seem to indicate their attitudes while in power.

The young woman, sitting away from her companion, a man maybe ten years older, feels the grit in the air sticking to her pale skin. She fidgets, attentive to the handbag on her lap. Her hazel eyes are large, sad, she has heavy eyebrows, and her hair hangs in dark-red, clumpy curls. She takes a small hand mirror from her handbag, checks her full lips, her nose, and wipes her cheeks and nose with a folded tissue.

"You look fine," her companion says. "Beautiful. As always."

He watches the back of the driver's head: the muscles of his medulla oblongata flex to a calypso beat on the car radio.

Oh God! Poverty is hell,
But don't mind – don't mind the smell
Cause everything – everything after here
Is wine and shine and is only sweet music you will hear!

She gazes out the window at the distant scattering of slums, in the last light, on the mountains rising directly behind the city. To the west of these, on other mountains – their green lawns discernible even from this distance – are luxury houses.

It is remarkable, she thinks. Everyone has a view.

She longs for rain. Its heavy wetness will cleanse the air and drown the sounds of the city traffic. Perhaps it'll erase, for a short while, her time and place. They are both something she can taste: car exhaust, mixing with the dead salt of dirty sea water, and the burning of the island, scent of its dry earth and trees reaching them all the way from the mountains, borne on wind like a reminder of what once was, of a time before fire.

History has brought her here, that and bad decisions: she looks over at one now: he's tapping his fingers on his knee, his hawkish face uneasy (or is it anticipation, she wonders)... He's still watching the back of the driver's head. The driver gestures now and then emphatically, left hand out of the window; sometimes he gets an obscene response. She swallows, feeling tiny grains make their way down her throat. She thinks of cold mountain streams; thinks of lying naked in them, drinking the water through her skin, while watching the cool green sway of trees above.

On the mountains, as the light fades, little dabs of orange flame become visible. With night, as on so many other nights during the first months of each year, the fires appear floating in the sky, like huge amber necklaces.

There is no other beauty but that and the young woman beside the man.

They stop at the port, at the ferry service that connects the island with another in the north. The taxi-driver, thinking they are tourists, tries to overcharge them. She glances at her male companion, brushes her hair out of her eyes and says to the driver, "Think we stupid, or what? Just because we white, you think we not from here."

The driver, a black man in his early thirties, says, "Eh-eh, hear she, Mistah. *Hear* she. And like she know the talk, too! I sure she could real pretty up my life. How much you want to give me, darlin'? How much?"

The driver has shifted around in his seat and is looking at them with an almost demented enthusiasm. Now they see he's drunk. He grins.

Her companion leans forward and drops a blue bill on the seat beside the driver. "There," he says casually.

"Tell Glen to improve the transport," she says.

He nods.

The driver removes the money and ignores them now, his little show over. They get out, taking two carry-on bags with them. Walking towards the boarding station, beyond which the massive bulk of the ferry looms, she smells diesel and, stronger here, the dead salt of the sea. Inside, standing in line, she begins to look around. The dull yellow lights, heat, and the scent now of sweat: she has a strong desire to leave everything within her vision; to levitate through and above the station, above the port into the grey, ash-scented air, and beyond it.

There are some tourists, mostly middle-aged and tired. A Mediterranean-looking man, wearing beige trousers and a light cotton shirt, about fifty and alone, joins the line opposite. The other passengers, many of them standing several feet apart, are moving toward either side of a check-in counter. The young man and woman take up similar positions, holding their carry-on bags securely but paying them no attention. They begin to speak quietly.

"How about him?" he asks her, giving a brief nod at the man in the light cotton shirt. "Seems pleasant enough."

"Sure," she says, with a smooth indifference. "Nice and fat."

He says nothing. Then: "He's a tourist."

She looks back at the Mediterranean man.

"We'll get there near midnight, like always," he says. "Then we'll just go straight to Glen's house. Nothing to worry about."

He is staring at the man.

"House. Sounds so funny – no, strange – to be talking like this. You'd think we owned one. A *house*."

"We'll have enough for one soon, well – a condo at least. But forget that," he says. "Think about him."

She thanks him for his advice.

"Stop it," he says.

Their tickets are stamped and torn by a sullen black woman at the check-in counter. Then they notice the Mediterranean man in the cotton shirt has disappeared.

She smiles. "You'll have to find someone else, my dear."

He watches her, irritated.

They board the vessel in silence. The dock lights and city lights brighten further as night deepens. On the sea the darkness has gathered massively; they sense the inevitability of facing it, but for now, on the aft deck, they watch it give full life to the vast necklaces of amber fires in the mountains.

"It's so beautiful," she says.

He notices the colour of the fires shows tints not unlike those in her hair, in certain light: an orange-brown gold, like the blaze of hazy sunsets over ravaged landscapes.

They are sitting near the stern.

"What do you think of that one?" he says.

"Where?" She turns away from the island.

"Leaning on the rail, to our left."

She stands up. "He seems okay. But chubby again. You like them like that, don't you?"

"We've done well so far."

"Of course, my dear," she says, doing a little skip and dance three-step. "And so much depends on the ability of my pussy. Pussy power," she says, with a giggle. Then: "Damn thing's itching. I shaved too closely."

"Stop it," he hisses. "He looks suitable."

But she retains the tone. "I feel so close to you at moments like this, darling. But why must they always be near middle-aged and porky? Get me a nice, young buck. Someone who can fuck me silly."

He doesn't reply. The ferry begins to move; there are vibrations along the railing. The island begins to shift, slipping. The second man moves away. Soon, the scent of decay and fire begins to lessen; there is a light breeze. The sea and night become attractive to look into. She tries to find stars, but he says she has to wait until they are far away from land.

In the rest room, handbag slung over her shoulder, she examines her face carefully, applies a rich flesh-tone lipstick, and lines her eyes lightly with black mascara. The ferry engine tremors everything she touches: the greasy pipes, the soles of her shoes (from there it travels up her legs, to the tips of her fingers, to the lipstick on her lips), the cling of her blouse, jeans, even the gold chain around her neck.

She leans over the sink, closer to the mirror now, but the age of it – cracks, spots, dust, signatures of neglect, like so much she has seen in her life – distorts her image, so she steps back. She angles her position to the mirror, and there, in the slant of clinical white light, she sees the inner place, that closest part of herself known only to her, nesting in her eyes.

Hello.

Transfixed by her own stare, she lifts the chain around her neck and clasps her hand over the medal. She keeps looking at her eyes and visualizes the miniature image, on one side of the medal, of a dolphin leaping from the water and an island with a single palm tree in the background. On the other side are the words: "Toward a State of Grace".

It is from him.

Ab imo pectore.

Outside, at the starboard railing, she rests her elbows on the cool iron: *Young Woman, Alone at Sea. Night.* The darkness of the sea is physical: the wind has texture, moist salt on her cheeks a constant anointing; and its sound is melancholy, sometimes whip-whistling shrilly around the rails, approaching grief almost.

They will cease these activities soon, he's told her. There is nearly enough money. And yes, we can get out. Glen knows he needs new recruits; we've become a little too familiar round here... No, I don't think he'll relocate us. We've done our time, been to the places, seen the sights, and been seen.

And the other thing?

Later she says to him, "Life is madness," and gestures at the wake, now the colour of starlight. "Yet you have this marvellous way of sorting everything out. You're a great organizer, you know; so creative. You should be in government."

"I suppose I could get involved, but it's dirtier than this. We'll certainly have enough money soon. It could be a good investment."

"Is Glen connected?"

He shrugs.

The Mediterranean-looking man they first saw on the dock reappears. He sits down on a bench near one of the sealed, elevated lifeboats, loosens his tie, and begins smoking.

"Look. He's waiting."

She turns around. "The porky man is back," she says. "I like it when they come. They quiver all over, like doves."

She starts across.

"Be careful," he says.

Animula vagula –

"He's an original: actually said no thank you. Told me he was happily married. Told him I was too – almost – but that you had a low sperm count and needed assistance. He seemed to believe that more than an offer of a good fuck."

"Sure he said no? He's looking over. See?"

She ignores him. "I can't wait to get to the house."

"I want you to go back."

"Not interested. I told you."

He appears to consider this for a moment.

"Okay, okay," she says. "Maybe he's surprised by my race. Nice middle-class girl fucking for fun. He must be very traditional, my love. A nice brown-skin might suit him. Oh... he's smiling now. Cute, isn't he? I wonder if he coos."

"Once he knows you're for real –"

"You seem to forget, darling, I'm a nice, university-educated girl who was once very –"

He grabs her arm. "Serena."

"You need me to do it, don't you?"

They are close, looking straight into each other's eyes, her face well below his. They remain that way, for about fifteen seconds.

She backs away from him. For a few moments, she seems sad. But then: "Yes, my love," and does her little three-step routine again.

"Go."

"Are *we* okay?" Her eyes have narrowed, the soft delicate skin around them tensing.

"Don't worry about that. Just enjoy it."

"Don't you like to watch any more? Or ask about it? You used to. Or do you just imagine it now?"

"I can't always look. You'd have to leave the curtain ajar or something, if there's one."

"You're such a funny man. It's too risky."

He waves her away. She goes, leaving him with both of the bags.

For about an hour he watches the dark sea. The wind and gentle sway of the ferry relax him. The island is lost to sight. He checks his watch, yawns, and glances upward. There, cast in a density he has never seen before, are all the stars anyone can imagine. Meteors occasionally cross the star-stilled blackness.

He remembers a time he enjoyed it so much that the heat from it made him dry mouthed and he needed water or a beer, preferably a beer – any alcohol, frankly, was better in the beginning. What was it then? It was fear and jealousy and erasing those emotions, and then it was something else he never left alone, never got enough of: exquisite, bright sweet pain burning in his heart and chest so much that after they played and he slept beside her he felt filled with all of the world: nothing could hurt him. But it never lasted. And he burned to know she'd done it again, to feel his veins and arteries expanding and his blood hotter than at any other time in his life so he became dry mouthed and drank more water during that time than ever before.

But it's something else now, has been for a while, and he's curious.

She's standing thirty feet away, leaning on a rail and looking out to sea. The stern light shows the curve of her face; her full-lipped mouth is solemn. He notices her hair: most of it is now held back; gold-red wisps play around her neck. Her gaze seaward is bright. She's put on a light amount of make-up. As he moves towards her, she shifts a little, and then straightens, blinking a few times.

"Trouble?"

He steps to her, close, is about to embrace her with his left arm around her shoulder when she moves away. He stops. Draws back.

When she turns to him, her eyes reveal nothing. "No. He was quite tickled by it all."

"Nice."

"No problem," she says, trying to reclaim her earlier energy. "There's never any problem, usually... Can we stay longer at the house?"

"Glen won't mind."

He reaches out for her hand, but she doesn't want him to touch her.

The wind is steady, cool and moist, and they listen to it.

It is morning and they are in the house. For a few moments, if she closes her languid eyes, she can imagine it's her place, and there is no Glen or him. In the bedroom upstairs she leaves the curtains open for light and sleeps fitfully for most of the day, sometimes staring out at the blue sea and the thinner blue of the sky. Her companion sleeps in another room, downstairs. Late in the evening, Glen arrives. He checks the weight and packaging of the parcels they've brought in the carry-on bags. Then they all have drinks.

Glen sits with his legs up on the couch in the living room that gives a view of the sea through a huge glass window behind him and raises his glass to them. He looks at her with casual lust.

The sea, from the height of the house on the hill, is a massive expanse of darkness, deeper than the sky.

"Glen," she says. "Are you with the government?"

Her companion looks over at her instantly.

Glen smiles and lifts his drink from the lamp-table beside the couch. The light catches the crystal glass of scotch as he says, "Darling, I am the government – part of it, anyway."

He is a friendly looking man, a bit portly, older than her companion, and his hair is greying in tufts around his ears. When he tilts his head back and gulps the drink, she sees the bump of his larynx jumping like the beating of a little heart.

ELUSIVE ARTHUR

SOPHIE WOOLLEY

There was no escape from the quantum barrage of moping exes. "You again!" said Lalla. "Whoever invented human teleportation should be shot." Her unsolicited ex dithered pathetically in the middle of her palatial reception room. He had apparently grown a fluffy new beard for the occasion and was dressed casually in a pair of old boxer shorts. His socks were very odd. "You didn't even make an effort!" Lalla shouted. The ex choked back tears, mumbled a self-pitying "sorry" and pinged off as suddenly as he had pinged on. Only the strange echo of his snivelling lingered. Sound always lagged behind.

Then Lalla remembered. Whoever it was that invented domestic teleportation *had* actually been shot – assassinated by a jealous colleague over some sort of irresolvable quantum ethics feud. Or so they said on sky. Good. Too bad the assassin didn't spill his coffee on the blueprint.

Teleportation was mainstreamed now and some nights Lalla couldn't roll over in bed without bumping into someone she knew. What was the point of living in a metropolis of millions if you couldn't even be anonymous in your own bed? Life had become very annoying. Friends and forgotten acquaintances kept pinging in to say hello in the middle of the night – they were all in different time zones. Teleportation was worryingly unregulated. She had a human spam blocker but it only blocked total strangers and it cost an arm and a leg. Good job she was fantastically rich.

Lalla flicked her hair implants and addressed Triff, her dog and trusty PA. "It's shit being popular." Triff swore in agreement and jumped up to lick her face. Lalla pressed the bridge of his nose and said "Off!" and he backed down. He was a good dog, modified to speak like a human and much more fun than a boring old robot. He was a scruffy little thing with cunning, wolfish eyes and an IQ of 203. Lalla patted him, gave him a dog treat, and returned to gazing out of the window of her 92nd floor, luxury flat-pack-build BioFlat. As she breathed on the bullet and laser-proof window, the view vanished. The sensors picked up the hunger on her breath and replaced the view with a gastromap of the world. She scanned across Europe, the Middle East and then Africa with her eyes, moving the gastro hybrid map views southwards, browsing for somewhere nice to go for lunch. Somewhere that accepted mongrel, talking dogs.

Triff trotted off to the balcony on the other side of the apartment. He wanted to have a go on the slides outside. Lalla's pad was connected to a sprawling slide network that served the upper echelons of London's docklands and Hackney C. If you went out for a pint of purewater, your feet never needed to touch the ground. Triff loved the slides and he wanted to go on them all the time, but Lalla only used them when they actually needed to go somewhere local.

Triff whined at the metal slidiness that twinkled enticingly in the relentless glare of the sun. He drooled at the glinting helter-skelter spaghetti network that crisscrossed the sky and skewered the rainless, orange smog below. Lalla's private slideway drove steeply downwards off the end of the balcony, twisted around in a bespoke loop-the-loop and then dipped gently to connect with Level 83, where people were queuing for the public slide to the shopping fields of Hackney C. Triff barked warningly at a low-flying private plane and then trotted back inside.

Lalla had given up on the idea of lunch abroad and was sucking on a local superfood readymeal in her office. She was working on secret plans for the overthrow of the SpecialMen, the organised multinational and genetically enhanced criminals who controlled everyday life, everywhere, in a very organised and intrusive way. It was early days, but Lalla had formulated the beginnings of a plan to weaken their powerbase in a devastating quantum strike that would spark revolution on a global scale. But she was getting nowhere with it today. The unsolicited ex had ruined her concentration. Despite his beard, he was still very handsome, and had a big penis. But he was always broke. Maybe that's what he was after – some more of her hard-won cash.[1] Fortunately Lalla was very tight, and made no apologies about holding onto her trillions. Like Triff always said: "If you give 'em a penny they'll ask for a pound". Lalla was saving her euros for her baby. Only she didn't have a baby and she still wasn't pregnant.

Lalla wanted a baby more than anything. She wanted one more than world peace. There was a big gaping hole in her life that could only be filled by having a proper baby – as opposed to buying a fake one from the tesco. But getting pregnant was tricky. Only the very special had babies. Fertile donors were increasingly rare and the availability of sperm was tightly controlled. Everyone's genetic codes were kept in a sealed vault under the sea, guarded by the SpecialForces and accessible only by the elite, inner circle of SpecialMen. The only way to get legally pregnant was to apply to the SpecialMen, but that meant waiting on hold to their call centre for six months and then completing a four-year pregnancy training course.

The only other way to get pregnant was to find a black market donor or strangerdad. Some women in desperation used teleportation and pinged around the world meeting potential strangerdads. But many were lecherous fakes. Most genuine strangerdads already had a thousand children and were starting to get bored of it all. Some were quite worried about inbreeding.

In the old days you could just get a secret baby off a donor and then flick him out of your life forever by changing your phone number and leaving town. But now, wherever you were, you were traceable. To make matters worse, strangerdads often turned out to be counter-corrupt SpecialMen who wanted a return on their investment. And Lalla had seen rumours of SpecialMen agents posing as potential strangerdads to clamp down on black market babymaking.

The way things were, getting pregnant and defeating the SpecialMen was no more than a pipe dream. Lalla threw a dart at the regulation, framed poster of Chief SpecialMan III on her wall and locked away her secret plans. She'd come a long way since her days as a call-centre worker with nothing but the odd holiday in the rain for fun. But now she was rich, she felt even more powerless. Money had not bought her freedom and the world was a mess. She wanted to do something to make everything better. But how to do it alone? There seemed to be no organised resistance any more.

In a doomed attempt to cheer herself up, Lalla clicked disconsolately through her old photo albums, projecting the images on her walls and wandering around the room. She had thousands of pictures of grinning friends, squeezing each other together in relatively happier times, before the SpecialMen had tightened their genetic grip on the world. But the photographs only increased Lalla's despond. Remembering being happy wasn't making her happy.

Maybe now was a good time to springclean the past. She clicked open her ex files and tutted at her collection of old boyfriend snaps. It was like looking at a series of fashion mistakes – could her tastes really have changed so much? The early exes were a mixed bunch of jokers and bohemians, the later ones handsome gold-diggers. She began deleting them but stopped short when she came across a long-forgotten image of one of her favourite people in the whole world: Arthur.

Her heart vaulted. It fell over inside her and she had to sit down and catch her breath. She looked at his picture and everything came flooding back. All of it. Her heart fell out. It fell on the table. It was flashing red. She put it back in. But there was no known cure for flashing red.

She tried in vain to wipe her nostalgia. She reminded herself how rubbish he was. It was just a photo. He looked like a bog-standard office worker, all waxed-up hairdo, cheap shirt, fat tie, grey trousers and computer-screen tan. When they'd first met he'd been a slideway technician, but later began job hopping and ended up managing a dubious online casino. Arthur was a bit of a directionless job slag, but she'd loved him all the same. She thought about what they'd got up to on the slides. About how she would always end up smelling of his cheap, retro hair wax. She gazed at his piercing, wolflike eyes and he smiled right back at her, out of the photo and back into her heart.

He wasn't an ex exactly. More of a "one that got away". In the days before the crackdown on reproduction, they'd had a three day fling. Lalla fell pregnant but aborted as soon as she received the message alerting her to her new status. It was a hard thing to do – and she regretted it now – but Arthur was anti-baby and didn't love her, and she was young and had lots of important parties to go to. The hardest part of it all was that she had fallen madly in love with Arthur for no apparent reason. At the time, she told herself it was just a phase, and that if she ignored it for long enough, it would go away. But it never did. Arthur went away, but it didn't.

Maybe he was still fertile. Maybe she could get a baby off him, with wolf eyes just like his. A piece of him to keep forever, a piece of him that would love her back. She clicked on another photograph which featured Arthur winking seductively at the camera as he drank a can of crack. She'd written a note underneath: "Only fuck it if it moves". That was Arthur's motto – a bit too broad in scope for some, but it summed him up, and he lived by it very well.

Lalla lost her reason and strode over to her teleporter. Triff sniffed the danger and ran to her barking: "Think before you ping!"

Lalla ignored him and checked her reflection in the mirror.

"You look beautiful", said Triff.

"Do I? I hope Arthur thinks so."

Lalla tapped Arthur's code number into her teleporter. Triff whined in dismay as he remembered Arthur's dog allergy and pungent hair scent.

"Arthur? But he's a dick."

Lalla shrugged. Triff was just an overeducated dog – what did he know about dicks? There was no time to lose, she had to see Arthur immediately and try and get pregnant off him. She had to catch him before he ran out of sperm or went insane and got married. It was a desperate world and more and more people were regressing every day. She stepped into her teleporter and closed her eyes like a child making a birthday wish. As she dissolved, she wondered where Arthur would be. Triff vanished after her.

They dissolved into a quantum transfer zone. Suddenly there were fifty of her. And fifty of Triff. All the Triffs were swearing at her telling her in many different ways not to do this to herself and asking for a go on the slides instead. There were suddenly five hundred of Lalla shouting back saying, "Back off Triff! I'm just popping by to say hi and then get a baby off him. I want a baby with eyes like a wolf!" Triff went quiet and looked away, all three thousand of him averting six thousand wolfish eyes – now ten thousand eyes anywhere but her. A million Triffs lay down wherever they were and covered their eyes with their paws until the madness was over.

They resolved.

Arthur was in New York propping up a drink in a tacky bar. Typical. Many of the customers were g-listers on drugs, filming themselves in compromising states of inebriation for syndication to sky. Arthur was busy gazing at a barmaid and didn't notice Lalla at first. She pretended she'd arrived the old fashioned way: "Of all the bars in all the world…"

"Oh God not that," he said.

"I wanted to see you."

"It's good to see you," he said. He was gorgeous. Older, redder, fatter, balder and uglier but he still had that thing. Against all the odds, he looked like his sperm still worked. She scanned the bar to check the coast was clear

"Are you alone?" she whispered.

"I am now, she just fuckported off to Hong Kong without me."

"Why?"

"I asked her if she wanted to go to bed."

"Nice try. Listen, I wanted to ask you something face to face."

"I'm not giving you a kid."

"How did…"

"You're the third one today. None of them want to go to bed though. Christ, it's all so impersonal."

"But there are hardly any donors any more, only SpecialMen. And besides –"

"Oh grow up Lalla, you never used to be like this. What's got into you? If you have a kid Lalla – mine or anyone's – I will never speak to you again. I hate kids; they're boring."

"Fine," she said, "but you might get lonely."

"I am lonely. Do you want to go to bed?"

"For no reason?"

"Yes! Lets go to bed for no reason."

Back at Arthur's slum shack in Mexico City, they shut the door on Triff and went to bed for no reason. They kept their clothes on because they were mad with long lost passion, or so she thought. Really, it was so he could make a quick getaway. In the middle of intercourse, Arthur flicked a switch on the bedstead, licked a sensor on his watch and dissolved mid thrust. He vanished without even a goodbye kiss, leaving her with her legs and arms in the air and a terrible void where his penis once was. Arthur had gone before he'd even come. What kind of pig fits a teleportation rig to his bed? What kind of pervert goes before they come? And she'd gotten so close to tricking him out of some sperm. Lalla curled up into a little ball and wept. Triff nosed open the door and jumped into bed with her.

"Don't cry Lalla," said Triff as he licked the tears from her face hungrily. "He's a slippery fish that Arthur, and I hate to say I told you so. Hey! What happened to your finger?"

Lalla held up her right hand and saw that her little finger was missing. "Woah, must have been a dirty teleport. Never mind, I'll get a new one from the tesco."

"That's the spirit," said Triff, "never cry over split digits."

Lalla managed a smile. "Sorry we shut you out Triff. I hope you weren't too bored."

"No worries, I teleported to the undersea genetic vaults and bribed the SpecialForce guards with a billion euros."

"Triff! You could have been killed!"

"Yeah I know it's dangerous, but they thought I was really cute. Anyway the good news is I've stolen Arthur's genetic coding, so now you can get pregnant off him without him finding out. And I know a black market geneticist who'll fix you up and fake the birth registration to make the baby look Special."

Lalla kissed Triff long and hard. He was a bad dog, but she loved him very much.

Footnote

1   The money was actually won by Lalla's dog in a freakishly cunning bet on the British weather. Rain is a rare occurrence in the UK but Triff successfully bet that it would rain on a certain date and won trillions of euros which he donated to his mistress, Lalla. See www.sophiewoolley.com for more details.

ESTRANGEMENT

AMRAN GAYE

He saw the notice for the competition on Tuesday, on one of the websites for aspiring writers. "We are accepting short stories", [it read], "incorporating the phrase 'global village', or in some way dealing with the theme". He thought about "the phrase 'global village'", and what it meant. The first impression that came was of a vast interconnected world, thousands of electric pylons on a cartoon globe, thick wires running between them, carrying the world's information. People everywhere in touch, any time, all the time, information descending like a mist over the world's citizens – but here the metaphor broke down. A mist-obstructed sight, kept people apart. Perhaps a cloud... but that too... Then he was called to his boss's office, and he mentally filed away the idea for later. His boss's computer had begun emitting mysterious and embarrassing sounds at random intervals, for no apparent reason. He thought perhaps it was a virus. No matter how many times he warned them about downloading messages from unknown senders they would not listen. The problem took up the rest of his day and he left work that afternoon in a dark mood.

As he sat in the back of a van on his way home, he thought about the competition again. There was the Internet – but what could one write about that that had not already been written? Then came a succession of ideas, each dismissed almost as soon as it arrived: a love story, with the lovers separated across two continents, able to communicate only through the net. Too clichéd, too unoriginal. A global disaster, leading to the destruction of a world that had become so interconnected everything spread almost instantly from one location to another: information, disease, death. An epidemic which would destroy almost all of civilization – narrated by one of the few remaining survivors. His unfixed gaze fell through the dirty glass of the van window on the human activity outside. He saw one man chase another, both laughing, their *kaftans* trilling silently in the wind. He saw a woman selling watermelons by the side of the road, letting passers-by taste before they bought, cutting neat squares with red, triangular undersides, and suddenly the idea that he would destroy the world (even if only in his fiction) felt foolish, absurd in the utmost. He was distracted by the apprentice, bent over in the cramped space of the van, getting up to ask for fare-money, and passengers breaking out of their vigil-like silences to reach into pockets and handbags.

At home that evening, his ex-wife dropped off the kids. After he had exhausted the conversational topics they shared – school, Ida's hairstyle, Kebba's football – he left them in the living room to watch DVDs, and went to his room. He went on-line, and was soon distractedly switching between conversations as he spoke to a dozen people at once, his laptop making a contented 'blimp' every time he received a new message.

After a while he got up to go to the bathroom, and on his return to the living room was drawn by its silence. He saw a strange sight: the kids scattered around the room (Ida on the sofa, Mose and Kebba on the floor), the TV off, the only sound the tap-tap of their thumbs as they sent SMS on their mobile phones, completely ignoring each other. Ida laughed as she read something off her mobile phone screen, and Kebba grunted without looking up. Each seemed to be in a different location, in different parts of the World, great distances separating them. They had perhaps been this way since he left them. He stood in the corridor, not making a sound, willing one of them to look up. It seemed suddenly to be of the greatest importance that they should notice him, as if he could only exist if they paid him attention. But they did not, and he thought: I will make a sound. I will cough. But his nerve failed as he thought about what he would say to their questioning looks. He turned and fled back to his room, back to the safety of his computer and its now-impatient bleeping, and his faceless friends waiting in other time zones.

That night, before he fell asleep, he decided he would write an apocalypse story after all, a sci-fi piece narrated not by survivors (there wouldn't be any), but by aliens aboard a spaceship come to conduct research on the planet. The next day after work (another tiring, virus-filled day), he started on it, fleshing out the aliens' story, searching for sentences which would show how different they were from humans, yet still retain the core of humanity which would make it memorable and worth reading. He worked late into the night. Finally, exhausted, he saved the file and went to bed.

On Friday he was informed by his boss that he would have to go to a village up-country to conduct a technical site survey for a potential partner. This happened once a year, and for the past three years he'd been able to weasel out of it by making excuses, so someone else from his unit was sent. But this time he'd come marching into his boss's office expecting another virus problem, ready with another polite-but-strict lecture on the dangers of downloading unsolicited emails, when his boss asked him to take a seat and given him the news that so nonplussed him he had not protested, or been able to deliver the excuse he had been working on for the past few months.

"Thank you for volunteering," his boss said, dismissing him, and it was only after he had closed the door that his heart sank over the prospect of a long, exhausting journey on the pot-holed and dusty roads, the heat, the mosquitoes, and the hundred other inconveniences which made travelling upcountry such a terrible experience.

He left on Saturday, at dawn. The road was as he had expected, if not worse. He travelled alone with the driver; their conversation dried up within the first fifteen minutes. After that there was the radio, music and intervals of the BBC World Service.

The sun rose, heating up the insides of the Land Rover. Every time they saw another car approaching they would roll up their windows. Even so, when he looked at the driver, and saw the dustiness on the man's face and eyebrows, it made him clear his throat as he imagined the gritty particles building up there too, until they would choke him.

They arrived in the evening, turning off the road at a hand-drawn signpost to "Nyanijaha Village", and down a faint trail bordered by tall stalks of corn. Now they had to raise the Land Rover's windows against the dust raised by their own passage. In the village he saw people stop their work to look up. The houses were made of mud, scattered, with no discernible plan to them. A donkey led by a child gave way to them as they approached. He saw a herd of dirty, lean sheep. These things were not strange – he had seen them even in the city – yet here they seemed to gain an increased vividness, as if reality here was sharper.

At the NGO building they were welcomed, and given rooms. There was no electricity, except for two hours at night. His mobile phone only got a signal when he stood uncomfortably in a particular corner of his room. He had brought two novels, one almost finished, and after he had done with his work for the day he retired to his room with them. By dusk he had finished both. He decided to go for a walk.

Outside the air was still warm. He waved at his driver as he passed him at the gate, drinking *attaya* with the watchman. He walked through fields of wild thyme. Everyone he passed greeted him and smiled. Their friendliness warmed him – so different from the busy, impersonal streets of the city. He came to a shop, a concrete building with a corrugated roof. A woman sat outside, selling groundnuts out of a calabash. Children played in the sand at her feet. A young girl sat on a bench next to her. He entered the shop and bought a few mints. Outside again, the woman smiled and spoke to him in rapid Mandinka that he did not understand. But he caught the word Banjul, and nodded, pointing at himself. I am from the Banjul, he told the woman, nodding vigorously. The girl laughed excitedly, her hands clinging to the bench. The woman spoke more Mandinka to him, but slowly. He replied, in Wolof, to the question he thought he had been asked. The woman nodded, grinning, and asked another question. Perhaps they spoke of different things, but it was a conversation, nevertheless, and soon both of them were laughing as heartily as the girl. He sat, on the bench next to the girl. She leaned an elbow on his lap.

He stayed with them until it began to get dark. Sometimes they would fall silent, happy in each other's company, returning the greetings of the people who came to the shop. He felt calm and still, like the hot, unmoving air. When he left, the woman gave him a bag of groundnuts. He reached into his pocket to give her money but she put her hand on his and shook her head. He smiled, and thanked her. Back in the NGO building, he fell asleep early, and slept better than he would have given the humid night air credit for. The next day he finished his work, and by midday they were on the dusty roads once more, headed home.

When his ex-wife dropped off the kids on Sunday evening they found him in the living room, with the TV on. He was half-lying on the sofa, so tired he could not sleep, not really watching, his thoughts elsewhere.

"How was your trip?"

"Not bad", he replied, and she smiled and motioned at the kids before heading back to her car. He waved them in, and sat with them in the living room. They sat politely in the straight-backed chairs, stiff in their wait for him to go to his room and leave them alone.

"So", he said from the couch, "What did you all do today?" Gradually he drew them out of their surprise, and their reticence, and they began to talk. He found a deepness he had not expected, beyond football and make-up and hairstyles: they spoke about politics and the government and career choices. His exhaustion helped, perhaps: he was too tired to erect the barriers that had sprung into place every time he'd tried to communicate with them in the past, too tired to get up and leave, too tired to do anything but meander on, from one topic to the next, listening with pleasure to their opinions. He felt a rising warmth within him, a feeling that mingled with the tiredness and made him give great sighs of contentment. He could not stop smiling. Once, Ida received a text message and he thought perhaps he had lost her – but she only glanced irritatedly at her phone before pushing it aside and continuing with the point she had been trying to make, her hands drawing figures in the air as she spoke.

They went on like this until there was a power cut, and as they sat in the dark and he went into the kitchen to look for a candle, they still carried on the conversation, shouted out through the darkness and the wall separating the two rooms. He came back and set two candles on a table in the middle of the room, and they gathered around it, the four of them. There was a pack of cards, and they played, two against two, switching partners after each game, changing positions around the table. They jested, laughed and teased each other. Mose caught Kebba cheating, and there was much laughter as he sheepishly brought out the cards he had been stashing beneath the table. At one point he realized that he did not feel tired any longer, as if he could sit up all night at this table, with these people. He thought of the groundnut seller and her daughter, and the feeling arose that this conversation was only a continuation of that one.

Too soon, his ex-wife came back to pick them up. He thought perhaps she had made a mistake and come too early – but it was the right time, and he took them out to the car, shielding the candle against the wind with his curled palm. After they were gone he went back inside, and lay on his bed, waiting for the power to come back on so he could go on-line. Yet a part of him wished for the darkness to continue, so he could lie untethered like this until sleep took him. He slept.

The next day after work he went back to his alien story. He read again what he had written, and the reading felt like a chore, and he had to force himself to finish it. I am not in the mood, he thought. I will write later. But his heart was not in it. He knew he would not touch that story again. He closed the file and sat before the blank screen. He still felt weary, yet cocooned within his weariness he felt a revelation waiting. He thought, I will write everything that has happened. Perhaps within the writing he would understand.

He created a fresh document on his laptop, and started to type:

He saw the notice for the competition on Tuesday...

MISSING

CATHERINE SMITH

"Here's your coffee, love." Helen places Iain's Dundee United mug on the windowsill. As usual, he's gazing down the long strip of garden, damp and bedraggled after the recent May rain, towards the compost heap. He looks up and smiles.

"Thank you," he says. "How kind. Have you seen my wife, please?"

It happens so often these days she should be used to it, but it's still a kick in the guts. He looks rather nice today, neat and dapper in his new green-checked shirt and navy Chinos from Marks and Spencer's; her birthday present to him, last week. She'd had a rare trip into town while Morag, the agency care assistant, visited to give him his weekly shower, clip his nails, shave him and trim his hair. Thankfully, he was always good as gold for Morag, who was used to people asking her daft questions, or not talking at all. Helen had enjoyed the unfamiliar bustle of crowds, even the bright lighting, and the smiling woman at the till who agreed that the weather was "pretty poor" for this time of year – as though, briefly, Helen had a normal life, did normal things. She'd helped Iain pull off the moon and stars wrapping paper and he'd regarded the new clothes with bewilderment, then ignored them.

She kneels next to him and takes his hand. "Iain," she says, "I *am* your wife. I'm Helen."

He pulls his hand away and scowls. His face, usually blank, occasionally twists into real hostility. "No," he says irritably, "no, I'm afraid you're mistaken. My wife is young and bonny.

Long chestnut hair. Very distinctive, her hair. I don't want to be rude, but you're an older lady."

She takes two slow breaths, like the doctor advised; in, out; in, out.

"I'm *Helen*," she says, "it's me, the same person. My hair went grey, like yours has. We both got older, love."

He shakes his head and sighs, folds his hands in his lap and stares out of the window. She knows it's hopeless, trying to explain; he doesn't remember anything she tells him, these days. She's lost him.

"Don't forget your coffee," she says, "don't let it go cold."

"Thank you," he says, "I will. And if you see my wife, please tell her to come home. My daughter and I are missing her. Will you tell her?"

In the study, she settles herself in front of the computer screen, logs on and takes a gulp of coffee. Two emails; one from Jennifer. And one from Anthony.

Of course she should open her daughter's message first, but Anthony's will bring her more pleasure, frankly; she and Anthony understand each other, despite never having met, whereas she and Jennifer might as well live on different planets. His subject title is "Baguettes and Builders".

Dear Scottish lady, here in the Dordogne matters proceed in their usual smooth manner. I shouldn't be too cynical or ungrateful – the weather's warm and balmy, we've had days of unbroken sunshine, which the brickwork drinks in and holds all day so that when you rest your hand on it, you get the most incredible warmth back, like a gift... and huge, bright blue skies with skittering puffs of white cloud... forgive me, I'm going poetic on you – but even with everything going on here, it's such a magical place, I can't help wanting to share it with you – I'm pretty sure you'd love it – our local town, Cadouin, has a wonderful fourteenth century church – deep, cool pools of shadow inside – and the streets are always full of laughing, olive-skinned children, and there's such a lovely smell of fresh coffee and watermelon... anyway, ha ha, back to reality. Yesterday morning, two builders – Jean Philippe and his son, also Jean-Philippe, to make life easier – came to start work on repairing the garden wall. Initially Clare became very agitated by their presence and demanded that I send them away. I managed to settle her in the living room with her jigsaw and Sauternes – she won't drink anything else these days, did I mention that?! – and made the mistake of popping round the back to clear the leaves off the pool. Suddenly aware of a great commotion; lots of shouting and Clare giggling in that way that means she's up to something very, very naughty. By the time I made it round to the front, I was greeted by both Jean-Philippes covering their eyes and Clare standing, topless, in the doorway, her bra and blouse tossed aside, shrieking with laughter and trying to shove a baguette up her skirt in a most unseemly manner... oh, dear. When I think of what my lovely wife was like, even five years ago – the term "ladylike" could have been invented especially for her. Or, as the French say, "genteel". Now she's terrifying hardy rustics with simulated sex acts with bread. Needless to say I had a hell of a day with her thereafter; took ages to pacify her, and she threw her jigsaw on the floor and told me what she needed to cheer her up was a trip to London. Immediately. All the usual accusations about keeping her from her family, who love her. Some days she remembers her parents are dead, but mostly she doesn't. Sometimes, I want to scream at her. This makes me a Very Bad Person, I know...

Helen imagines Anthony holding Clare, soothing her as she raged and sobbed. When they first became correspondents they'd exchanged images – she was proud of herself for working out how you got the photos off the camera and onto the computer, and had sent her one of herself and Iain at his retirement party in the dining room of the White Hart hotel, surrounded by his colleagues, a glass of Glenfiddich in his hand. They'd both looked happy, relaxed; she'd worn a lilac linen dress which made her eyes look very blue and he'd looked younger than sixty-three – in good shape, and his hair still thick. A respected Science teacher, head of department at the best school in the city, surrounded by friends and col-leagues, looking forward to a well-deserved rest after all those years in the classroom; he was planning to buy a telescope, he told everyone that night, take up astronomy seriously; time to look upwards, and out. Speeches from the head teacher and from Roddy McLeod, the ex-pupil who now ran the Chemis-try Department at Edinburgh University, talking with such enthusiasm and affection about Iain's lessons; the after-school Science club he ran all those years. Iain had looked straight into the camera, which she'd given to a friendly waitress, and he'd beamed; he hadn't been angry that night, or worried, or weird. Helen hadn't been on tenterhooks, then, waiting for him to do something embarrassing – turn on the bar-staff, maybe, and accuse them of short-changing him, or asking Valerie Innes how her husband, who'd been dead for five years, was enjoying his golf.

And Anthony had e-mailed a picture of himself and Clare outside their immaculately converted French barn, the stones washed pale gold in the sunlight. Anthony, the ex-film producer, still handsome in his late sixties; fragile, wasp-waisted, ex-ballerina Clare, her bobbed hair still pretty; both of them smiling into the future. Helen had done a Google search on them, feeling slightly voyeuristic, but thrilled when it worked – turning up articles and photographs. The Beaumonts, the golden couple with their riverside house in Henley, their legendary parties – a full jazz band on the patio, playing long into the night; the endless champagne. Now, Anthony had told her, Clare jumped at sudden noises, couldn't stand music of any kind; often walked round the house at midnight, checking for spies, refusing to eat because the Mayor was poisoning her food.

Helen takes a sip of coffee; it's lukewarm, unappetising. She thinks, fleetingly, how wonderful it would be to sit outside a French café under a sun umbrella, wearing a cotton dress and sandals, sipping really good, strong coffee, watching the world go by.

She returns her attention to the screen.

All very gloomy; forgive me for dumping this, but you are the one who understands and never judges. My dear Confessor. How's life with you? Must away and dress Clare; she has a hospital appointment this afternoon and that requires her best dress, full hair-do, make-up and manicure, or she refuses to get in the car. Courage! A xxxx

Helen rereads the message and presses 'reply'.

Dear Anthony, I have to tell you that our weather is being very Scottish – or 'dreach', as we say – damp, drizzle, the odd hiatus where we throw aside our raincoats and brollies! – the baguette incident sounds distressing but I must admit to seeing the (darkly) funny side. Will the Jean-Philippes ever recover? Will the British be banned from retiring to the French countryside? Life with Iain is a bit bumpy at present; no attempted seduction of builders, but when I took him to Tescos yesterday he became very excited because he thought he'd seen our daughter Jennifer stacking shelves. A nice wee girl of sixteen or so, not unlike our Jennifer at that age I suppose, but when I told him Jennifer was forty and had been living in New York for the past fifteen years, he was having none of it. Then he tried to persuade the young girl to come home with us and revise for her Highers; offered to dig out some old exam papers. Imagine the commotion; how we didn't get chucked out I'll never know. The worst of it is, as you say, the lack of dignity. Can I say how much I hate this vicious bloody illness – are we still allowed to hate, when we're bombarded with all this nonsense about positive outlooks? I can't feel positive any more.

She blows her nose, sharply; don't give in to self-pity, she warns herself, that way madness lies. And anyway, there just isn't room for two mad people in the house. Everyone says you have to maintain a robust sense of humour, take one day at a time. Learn new skills. Like the Internet, with its forums for people like her. And Anthony. She types.

I thought these years would be the best, but the man I loved has gone missing. Sometimes I feel as though I'm living with a sixty-nine year old toddler whose mind has been abducted by sadistic aliens. I know I'm mixing my metaphors, but if Alzheimer's was a dog I'd take the mangy brute out and shoot it!

Her fingers rest on the keys. In one of his earliest messages he'd said, The world has shrunk, dear Scottish lady, and we can have friends anywhere we choose, at the touch of a few buttons. Friends. Yes, he was, these days, very definitely her *best* friend; most of her old ones – the face-to-face women she'd known and with whom she'd taught in primary schools for years – seemed less and less willing to spend time here, now that Iain's sudden mood swings and inability to recognise people he'd known for years, made any contact such hard work. And the few trips she'd made to the local support group had been dismal; a draughty Church hall, orange plastic chairs, lukewarm tea and Iain wandering off half way through to 'test' the light switches. No, thank you. She's closer to this man who lives in another country, whose past is very definitely another country; whose distance is only physical. She types:

My dear Anthony, could we, as friends, have an e-hug? And – if this is possible – love to Clare, and plenty for yourself. Thank you for the courage. I feel more and more in need of it! A demain, mon ami, H xxx

She hesitates again. A hug. Is that too forward? And *love*; that's a strong word.

Sod it. She's more and more convinced that honesty is the best policy. Except with her husband, for whom the truth is so often incomprehensible and cruel. She presses *Send* and feels lighter.

Jennifer's message is short, perfunctory, as always. She's been insanely busy. She hopes Dad likes the silver cufflinks; she got them from Bloomingdales. Helen feels the bile rising, burning her chest and throat. Unfortunately, she types, your father doesn't really have much call for formal wear these days. And if you weren't such a thoughtless cow you'd have realised that. She stares at the screen. Jennifer, with her New York apartment, her endless launches and functions; the annual visit home, a snatched week in June. Last time was particularly bad; she and Iain sitting opposite each other in silence, with Jennifer clearly appalled at his vacant silence, his agitated tappings and random wanderings, his sudden, rambling lectures on quantum mechanics or relativity.

Then she deletes the message and types, **They were lovely, thank you. I hope they didn't cost too much.**

Later, she stands in the kitchen with *The Archers* on in the background – for years, they'd listened to it together, before he became confused about who was who and why there were cows bellowing in the background – cutting Iain's pork chop into tiny pieces, and puts a spoonful of mashed potato on the side. No point giving him vegetables at the moment; he either ignores them or tips them onto the floor. Iain sits quietly at the table, looking around him as though he has no idea where he is.

"Here you are, my love," she says, placing the plate in front of him and tucking the serviette under his chin. "Are you hungry?"

He shakes his head. "I've had dinner already. Jennifer made me meatballs. And spaghetti. My daughter. She's a clever girl. Have you met my daughter?"

"That wasn't today. That was another day." She keeps her voice calm and cheerful, gives him his knife and fork. "Today we're having pork chops. Your favourite."

"My favourite?" He looks forlorn, this elderly, disorientated stranger she's married to, nurses, feeds, and occasionally wants to abandon.

"Have some of this, love." She picks up the gravy jug tips it over the meat; it pools around the mash. He stares at it, fascinated.

"What's that brown stuff?"

"It's gravy, Iain. Lovely. You love gravy."

"My wife used to make gravy," he says, spearing a piece of meat and then chewing. "Have you met my wife?"

"Yes," she says, "several times. She's very beautiful, isn't she?"

He beams at her and begins shovelling in food. "Very, very beautiful," he agrees, and she tries not to mind that he's eating with his mouth open and mashed potato is sticking to his chin. "And I have a daughter. Did I tell you I have a daughter? My daughter made me meatballs today."

After dinner she mops round his mouth, settles him on the sofa, takes out the photograph albums and sits next to him.

"Who's that, now, Iain?" she asks gently, showing him a picture of himself from 1971, standing behind a bench, Bunsen burner flaring in front of him, flanked by two smirking teenagers, a boy and a girl, holding up empty test-tubes. It had been taken for the school yearbook; she remembers him laughing about it when he came home that evening, about how bloody ridiculous the whole thing was – and yet she knew he hadn't really minded; he loved that school, those kids. He loved teaching. He seemed taller then, with good, broad shoulders; his white lab-coat sat well on him.

He shakes his head. "I'm afraid I've no idea," he says politely.

"That's you, love."

He frowns and studies the photograph for a full minute, then sighs.

"Oh, I don't think so. No, I don't think that can be right. I don't have a coat like that. Do I?"

"You used to."

"Where's my wife?"

"Here." She flips the pages and finds a photograph of the three of them, having a picnic on Gairloch beach. August, 1974. Little knots of holidaymakers sitting round on rugs and towels; in the background a dog shaking a clump of bladderwrack in his mouth. Iain looks relaxed, lanky in his baggy shorts and sweater; and herself in a red shirt and jeans, her long dark hair in a pony tail; Jennifer pouting at the camera, cute as a button in yellow shorts and tee-shirt.

"Look, this is us. All of us."

I *was* beautiful, she realises suddenly, and the knowledge of it is shocking. And I looked *young.* And I'm not old now, I'm sixty-seven, that's not *old;* I just *feel* old when I'm with Iain. Not when I write to Anthony. Anthony makes me feel –

"That's my wife! There's our wee girl, our Jennifer!" He sounds delighted, grabs the album and smoothes his thumb over the photograph, again and again; as if, by rubbing, he might bring them all back.

Two days go by without a message from Anthony.

Helen checks her inbox four times a day. On the second day, the nurse visits and checks that Iain is taking all his medication. She talks about him as if he isn't sitting there.

At night, Helen can't sleep. She stares at the ceiling, and wonders what Anthony is doing. If her message, her request, has frightened him off. If her world, so expanded by his friendship, is about to close in on her again.

On the third day, she drives Iain to the Day Centre, hangs his coat, hat and scarf on a peg and guides him to a chair. He sits obediently and seems content enough when a young man in a grey tracksuit tells him that today a lady with a guitar is coming and they're all be singing, won't that be fun? He stares at his shoes and says nothing when he's asked for a favourite song.

"He hates singing," Helen wants to say, but doesn't. He used to hate singing – but that was when he was himself. Now, who knows?

She drives home and checks her inbox.

She reads it three times.

Dear gentle Scottish lady, terrible news. Clare was admitted overnight for tests, escaped from the nurse the when she wasn't looking and fell down two flights of stairs. Currently on life support but not for long. You will understand how I feel. It's dreadful. Love, A xxxx

Helen feels sick. She presses her forehead to the cool, dark screen. She types:

137

I am so, so sorry. Take care of yourself. Love, Helen. xxxx.

Helen's own life feels shrunk again; shrunk just to herself, Iain, a lost past.

I do understand, she thinks. I understand that you feel bereft but also liberated; so glad you don't have to watch her suffer any more. I won't leave you. Don't leave me. Keep writing.

That night, as she tucks Iain into bed, he whispers, "May I tell you something?"

"Of course," she whispers back.

He takes her hand and rubs his thumb over her wedding ring.

"Sometimes I look at you," he murmurs, "and think you're very nice, even though you're old. But I don't want to mess my wife about, you see. That wouldn't be right. I do miss her so much, you see."

She sits on the bed and smoothes the hair from his forehead. She imagines Anthony, combing Clare's thinned grey hair one final time; making her beautiful.

Two deep breaths. In, out; in, out.

"I know," she says, kissing his cheek. "I know you do. I'm sure, wherever she is, she misses you too."

CYCLE CHAIN ACID

RAHUL MITRA

Satish's mother told everyone he was a "nice boy", even when he grew tall like a palm tree and shaved until his razor went blunt and his face looked like he'd been through a barbed wire fence. His mother continued to say how nice he was, although he secretly watched his neighbour's young wife take a bath, cheated in tests, stole from his mother and carried a switchblade. Looking at his blank face you couldn't tell he was so tightly wound up, wrenched by all that pent-up anger, ready to slash with that spring-loaded knife he carried. It was not too difficult to recruit him.

In 1985, Satish and I ran a successful ganja-selling operation in our college in Hyderabad. I discovered the ganja business in the maze of the alleys on the darker side of the *purana pool*, a few kilometres from my apartment. It was a bright May afternoon. The paved gullies were empty, as if a curfew had been imposed by the mere presence of the police station in the vicinity. A window in the Kali temple wall, next to the police station, creaked open and a hand shot out. I peered inside. Suddenly I had a packet of ganja in my hand. I paid ten rupees for it and later sold it in the college as *Kali Special* for over 200 rupees.

My business spread by word of mouth. Satish with his switchblade became the obvious muscle and I the brains of the operation. Together we did all we could to keep up with the demand.

I was in the café drinking *chai* when a short wrestler sort of guy with pit-bull jaws and glassy eyes and a permanently crazed look loomed over my table and gripped my hand until pain shot through my knuckles. He seemed strung out. I tried to withdraw my hand. He tightened his grip.

"You know who I am?"

"I take it you want a discount?" Every friend of a friend felt entitled to a price cut.

He smiled, let go of my hand and kicked the chair in front of mine and sat down. "I am Surender."

I suddenly connected his face to his body and felt queasy. Satish had mentioned Surender and his powerful enemies. Rumour was that the leftist student union members had made several attempts to kill him, but Surender had overpowered his assailants and even maimed them.

"I heard your business is good. Not bad." He smiled. "Of course, you know I need my *baksheesh.*"

I looked up quickly.

Surender nodded. "Ah! It is the usual. Fifty percent," he said, lighting a cigarette.

"Fifty percent? I thought…"

"Well whatever you thought was wrong," he cut me off, waving his hand like a cricket umpire declaring a four. "If I have to chit-chat with the inspector from that Kali temple station, you owe me seventy percent."

I smiled at him and wisely didn't reply. I never messed around with the street dogs.

Surender ground his cigarette on the table top, flicked the butt to the side and walked away without looking in my direction.

On the days that followed, everywhere I looked in the college I saw Surender's smug face, with its insane look, eyes popping out, on banners that screamed in bold letters: *Vote for Surender Annah for President.* I suspected he'd win the election just by intimidation. The opposing candidate, backed by the leftist union, seemed wired, with a gaunt face, as if he was battling sudden withdrawal. I didn't think he'd be any better. Everybody in the college had some agenda.

The elections were a week away and Surender got busy doing whatever he did to bully the general population of our college. When he remembered me, he sent messages.

"Surender will break your kneecaps with a cycle chain and burn them with acid," one of his *chemcha* told me. I shrugged, though the awful feeling inside my gut told me the threats were not idle. With the elections ending the following week, I knew I didn't have much time.

I decided to strategize with Satish.

"Surender? Not good," Satish said nodding his head. "We need to do something serious. Let's meet this evening."

We usually met in the café on the YMCA grounds. Every evening student groups hung out there to smoke and chat. The topics changed from table to table, increasing in complexity quite randomly, from movies to street agitations.

On my way, watching the blur of lights on the road and hearing the horns, I waded through the crowds on the footpath. Neons glittered, advertising all the things I couldn't buy. My eyes fell on the legs of a twenty-something model on the billboard in skimpy, expensive clothes. I thought of Radha's smooth, shiny legs, slowly rising up and up until they ended in the dark shiny mass of hair. I lit a cigarette, changed my direction and began the long walk to her house.

The maddening sounds of horns began to fade and my nerves relaxed. I turned right by the Cricket Stadium into a street slick from overflowing drains. Apartments with peeling stucco and darkened with black grime from years past were packed tightly in the narrow street. It was a place where mothers hoped they would marry their daughters for little dowry and fathers expected to reel in as much dowry as possible for their sons. Light flickered from the occasional TV. There were shouts of a male voice, followed by blows and a woman's sobbing. I stopped.

Kali began her death dance in my head. I remembered the exact time my mother died. It seemed just a moment ago that I smelled pungent curry from our kitchen. We lived in a small rented house in a *basti* bordering the slums, on a small crowded lane where privacy existed only if you pretended it did. No one 'ever' heard the shouts and arguments – except for us kids. We played marbles on the street to get away from all the rage many of our fathers showed as a side effect of their alcohol intake. "Run, Kika," my mother would order, as soon as she saw my father wobbling in through the front door. One night when I was just completing my seventh grade, I ran into the back alley and sat behind the kitchen.

"You call this food?" my father shouted.

I heard the loud clang of the steel plate hitting the slate floor. Every time I heard the blows that followed his shouts, I felt sick in my stomach with fear. I wished my mother had run into the back alley with me. It was quiet all of a sudden. Then I heard her fall. I hurried back into the kitchen.

She lay on the floor, looking up at the ceiling. I thought her hair was moving by itself, until I saw the darkness of the blood creeping onto the floor from the side of her head.

"Kika," she said weakly. I sat next to her and held her bruised hand. She turned with difficulty and looked at me. Her eyes had drained of energy. She tried to say "run" before she closed them. I knew she'd never open them again.

My father walked away. Later, as my mother's body burned in the graveyard, my father stepped close to me. His mouth stank of the VAT 69 whiskey he loved so much. "She fell on her head," he said.

I turned and ran into the alley behind our house. I cried until it grew dark. I fell asleep there until my father grabbed me and pushed me into the house. We moved to an apartment complex two days later.

For years, I woke with visions of my mother lying on the floor, her eyes bleeding, asking me to leave. *Kika, run! Kika, run! Kika, run! Kika, run…* she whispered. I still lived with my father, but we hardly spoke to each other. Maybe one day I'd run across the bridge.

I shook my head to clear the buzzing. Lights swayed gently, as if bobbing on a boat floating freely down a river. Images of Radha came slithering, going in circles around my head.

142

The first time I saw her was when she parked her mustard Vespa in the college. She licked her thick lips leaving them wet and shiny with spit and pulled on her panty that I imagined rode up all the way. She brushed past me swaying gently, with a knowing smile. I followed her pulling on a sweet Kali Special rolled into a nice tight thick stick. We ended up in the shadows of our college's Hall of Fame.

It was a bright Wednesday morning, slanting golden rays danced on the roof just above her head. We attacked each other with our mouths as the Principals in *Nawabi* portraits watched with their eyes popping out of their ornate frames. She didn't slow down one bit, until the wall clock rang loudly. Radha wiped her mouth, kissed me goodbye and said, "Kika, you taste funny", and left me spent. I had to drag a whole stick of ganja before Kali kicked me with a buzz. It went on with her when and where. Pure love. No sugar coating. The kind that others pretend to be in, the only kind Radha would ever be in with me.

Radha, like me, came from a lower middle-class family. Her father worked as a clerk in the Secretariat. Her mother was not educated. Her family was a little better off than mine, since they had their grandfather's three-storeyed house. Radha's room was on the top floor. Sometimes, when she looked at the billboards, I saw desperation in her eyes. The kind that said – I want more.

I climbed the old bridge spanning a noisome sludge that once was a river. The din of the traffic turned to the incessant hum of people caught in the humdrum of life. Same and same. Through and through. Day and night. I crossed the bridge where the wife-beaters smiled respectfully, dope-sellers stared hopefully, pimps showed their whores, whores scratched their crotches, rickshaw-pullers looked for a fare, beggars waited for a coin to fall, thrill-seekers furtively peeped and police constables watched with bored eyes. What if one day the wife beater bought some dope, screwed a whore, and forgot his money? What if the pimp kicked him in a fit of rage and the constable, hearing his screams, came running and joined the pimp in the kicking – as soon as the pimp told him he wouldn't get his bribe because the wife-beater didn't have any money. They'd leave the wife-beater in a puddle of blood. What if late in the night the beggar gave some of his coins to the rickshaw-puller, who took the wife-beater home? What if the wife-beater got up the next day and did it all again. It'd go on and on like one gigantic diorama spinning inside a glass jar.

I lit a cigarette, took a drag and coaxed the grime from my neck with my index finger and thumb, shaping it into miniature black earthworms. I turned off the bridge into another lane reeking of garbage, behind a mechanic's store, and continued by sheer instinct into a maze of gullies filled with small houses, coming by turns and twists to a dead end and the unpainted brick and cement apartment complex with political graffiti and piss marks all over its walls. I scaled the wall and climbed the back stairs and waited on the parapet from where I could see her in the apartment just six feet away.

Radha.

At 8 pm, like clockwork, she came out of the shower, hair in waves probably smelling of *Lemony Lux*, wrapped in a white towel, without seeing me watching her, not dropping the towel – making me feel maybe she saw me after all. She sat for a long time in a plastic chair in front of a mirror, powdering her face, neck and her smooth skin, gently rubbing with her long fingers. She then turned and looked at me. I jumped onto her balcony and entered the room through the door she'd left ajar. She got up and closed the door, killed the light, slowly dropped the towel, and fell back on the bed. I dove in. I heard nothing but her moans until I almost blacked out and the street noise woke me up.

Radha was still naked. She sat on the edge of the bed and gazed into the darkness outside. "I saw him yesterday."

"Who?"

"Surender," she said. "Just outside on that parapet from where you jump. He was staring at me." She said folding her hands over her breasts.

"Are you sure?" I already knew the answer. Then I asked what was really worrying me. "You were dressed? Right?" My face began to heat up as I imagined Radha walking out of the

144

shower and tossing her towel on the bed and sitting naked by the mirror and powdering herself.

Radha broke out crying loudly.

"What happened?" Images burst in my mind.

"He came in. I didn't have time to cover myself. He grabbed me by my hair. He said he would do the worst I could imagine if you didn't give him what he asked. He showed me a bottle of acid."

"I'll kill that bastard," I shouted. I got up and pulled her closer. She pushed me away.

"I am scared, Kika."

Anger burst out of my every pore. I jumped off the bed and pulled my clothes on. My throat was dry. I slammed the door and jumped onto the parapet of the adjacent building.

By the time I reached YMCA, it was about 10 pm. I was seething with anger. Satish was sitting at a table in the corner of the café. I pulled a chair out and sat down.

"You look pissed off at something."

"That bastard, Surender."

"I said I'd deal with him," Satish said.

"He just about raped Radha and threatened to burn her with acid."

"What the fuck? We have to get this fucker now." He took out his switchblade. "I've told you several times before. He is not like the others we have dealt with. Surender is a *goonda*. He lives by intimidating others. We should do the same."

"How? You told me that he maimed the leftist group members who attacked him."

Satish thought for a while. "We could ambush him behind his favourite café in the old city. He usually drinks beer with the owner until midnight. We could get him in the alley he uses as a shortcut to his house. I could fucking stab him. He'll remember that for the rest of his life."

As soon as I saw Satish's eyes, I knew he meant it.

"What if it fails?"

"It won't." Satish flicked his switchblade many times, making swishing sounds.

"What then? You think he'd be scared of us? He'd kill us both."

"Don't think so. He probably won't even mention that he got stabbed. It'd be bad for business. If it fails, we can always talk to my friends in the leftist union. Leave it to me. It'll work. Let's have some beer now." Satish motioned to the café owner.

We drank into the night, preparing to implement the plan the very next day. By the time Satish left, I was sure it was a bad idea. The problem with Satish was once he started something, he wouldn't stop. I always handled him carefully, as if he was a pot of water at boiling point, ready to explode if shaken. That night I recollected all the violent fights that Satish had got into at college. He was lucky that no one had died. I hoped his luck would continue.

Sun was rising like a bleeding orange smeared over the horizon as I headed home. As I crossed the bridge I saw the dope-dealer, the pimp, the whores, the beggar, the rickshaw-puller and the cop, all animated and crowded at the mouth of the alley. I went closer.

"What happened?" I asked one of the women.

The pimp stepped in. "What do you think, brother? College is very violent. I keep telling Leela here that she is safer here with me than there."

I moved closer. The cop stopped me. "Go on. Keep moving."

I was about to turn away when I spotted a bottle a few feet to the side of the alley. It looked like one I had seen in the chemistry labs for storing acid. "Surender."

"Who?" the cop asked quickly. "You know this guy?"

"Who?"

"Look in there."

I pushed my way into the alley. There in the shadows lay a body.

"Somebody hit this guy with a cycle chain and poured acid on his face. What a way to die," the cop said.

The disfigured face was all blood and torn skin with pieces of bone sticking out of it. I turned around and threw up.

"You know him?"

"Surender." I said, spitting out acid vomit. "He's from my college."

"College students. You kids are putting criminals to shame," said the cop, and motioned me to move on.

As I left I saw a bloody switchblade a few feet away. What ever was left in my gut came running out. I threw up again.

Later in the evening I went to the YMCA. It was deserted. I sat in the café and drank *chai* waiting for Satish. I didn't think he'd go ahead with the plan. But knowing Satish, I should have made sure he reached home. He probably met Surender by accident, and must have attacked. I felt responsible for the death. I was angry at Satish. Then the thought of Satish telling the police that I made the plan with him came to my mind. *Would he say that?* Fear set in. Images flashed. Police beating Satish brutally in the prison. He looked just like Surender with his skin torn, eyes swollen and covered in blood. He started shouting my name.

I wanted to warn Satish not to talk to anyone about Surender or anything related to him. I waited for him until 9 pm. He didn't show up. I went to his home. His mother stuck her head out the window and asked me to leave. Just like that Satish vanished from my life.

I tried to run across the bridge, hoping to get away from it all. But the bridge I wanted to cross had burned so long ago that I was left in the sludge. Surender's death made it to the last page of the newspaper with a small headline saying that a politically motivated fight had lead to the killing of a college student. I spent paranoid days and nights but the police never came to question me.

I showed the headline to Radha.

"What were you involved in with him?"

"Nothing. I didn't know him at all."

"Why would he threaten me then?" she asked.

I didn't reply. Looking back, that could have been the exact moment when things between us cracked. She began to ask me to leave early and then one day, asked me not to come to see her at all. Strangely, I didn't feel devastated. Eventually, when I saw her at the college with a guy in a car, I told myself that it was just the car she was interested in.

I was running inside a glass jar like a fish, seeing the same things over and over again, until one day, about five years later, in the dead of the night, Satish appeared suddenly at the YMCA. At first I didn't remember his face. He seemed calmer and a bit rounder.

"Hello, Kika." He extended his hand to shake.

I didn't.

"Surender died the way described in the papers – in a fight with the leftist student union," he said as if nothing else had happened in our lives since then. "But when my mother heard about Surender's death, she immediately transported me to my uncle's house in Bombay. He sponsored me to study in America. I tried to write to you, Kika, but my mother said I shouldn't."

I had thought of a million ways to react if I ever saw Satish again. I couldn't recollect any of them. I stood there staring at him.

Satish sat and ordered us beer. "Old times, eh?"

I drank the beer silently.

"I started a new business in America in January 1990. I want to start a branch in Hyderabad," Satish said. "Your business skills are just what I need in a partner."

"What is the business?"

When he replied, it didn't make much sense.

"What is the internet?" I asked him.

TEN DAYS COUNTING SLOWLY

JENNIFER BRADY

Day 1

So, this is our holiday resort. And here is the residents' beach upon which a man in Speedos wrestles with a sun-lounger. The legs will not unfold. He thumps belly down on it anyway, his arms disappearing into the sand. He may well be the man who chooses me later, despite the woman. And here she is, all holiday breasts and wet hair, which she now rings out on the sole of his foot, for a bit of a laugh, and what fun! He reaches behind him and a rump of fat gathers on his left shoulder-blade as he latches a claw firmly around her ankle. She shrieks, straddles his buttocks, bastes his spine with oil. There are muffled noises of approval from him, laughter from her. It is all working. It is great. She is making, as most women do, a *job* of making the holiday a success.

And a success it will be.

I am that woman.

I am that woman with that man.

Day 2

And I assume most couples are like this?

"Michael? This is *my* side of the bedroom. This, (point, point) is *yours*."

"I hear ya, I hear ya," he says to the remote control.

He is looking for whatever channel it is on Latin TV that has the horny goodies for free.

"Damn thing," he says.

The screen will not produce a picture. The screen will only produce options that say 'no signal' when he presses the buttons.

Or, most couples are like this when the gleam of unification has gone.

Michaelandclaire, doubleincomenokids are back to being Michael.

And Claire.

Five years ago, I did not shudder at the sight of his athlete's foot cream. Now, I feel discomfort to the point of nausea at the open display of remedies that allude to a rot of any kind.

Day 3

Because? You can't smear good germs on decay and make it better. And what about the infidelities? Not only the ones we know about, but those which we don't. Did he, or did he not, have sex with the teenager in the yeehah hat in Paros while I was laid up with an infectious eyelid? Did I, or did I not, have an affair with the Safari guide in South Africa while he was rigid in a hotel room with an ingrown hair? And these are only the holiday detours.

Okay. Say we wanted a baby, abandoned the thought of marriage, skipped ahead to the main issue, *progeny*, do you think I would catch this wilting bull at the perfect moment of my own fading cycle? Because something happens to a man when he has passed a certain age. The prostate loses potency. He becomes, perhaps, a 'nicer guy', flaccid even. I too am pushing forty and feel the pipe and slippers draw near.

I sit on the balcony with a bottle of airport tequila, a shot glass for decency, and the more I drink, the more I am able to sum it up: some couples will never end up together and, out of those, the ones who have no courage end up 'ending-up-not-together', slowly. Riddle-me-ree. This could last a lifetime.

The sun nods its fat head over whatever ocean I am looking at, and wouldn't you know it? The world is rosier on the other side, just as it was rosier here when I was home. From the bedroom, Michael shouts, "It's fucking analogue!"

Day 4

The bedroom is his. The balcony is mine, and it is here where I sit and drink and watch. He sprawls on the fault line of the mattress zipper snapping like a dog at aeroplane treats he throws in the air for the challenge. He has tucked these secret eats away in a candid moment of foresight, despite the nausea he experienced on the flight. In between munches his mouth falls ajar.

This is it. This is what the end is. Looking at someone you love and seeing someone you hate.

He sucks his breath in and redirects a belch through his nose. He yawns and scratches his balls. His hand rests on his penis.

The thought of taking it in my mouth.

Yet, that I will do at some stage before the ten days are up. I turn my attention to the beach and what do I see? Another couple, of course. Too happy to bear. This time, the man sits on the edge of the jetty. The woman sits behind him, her legs spread in a V around him, her toes skyward, agonisingly graceful. This is the way a dancer sits as if moments of repose are and should be a ballet exercise. The man might be skimming stones, if the beach was of that ilk, but it is not. As it is, he imagines the leapfrog of his aim, and his hand is slightly closed on a nonexistent pebble, his wrist twitching rhythmically. From behind they are a monster-match of collusiveness. But up close, who knows? They may not be not touching at all.

Day 5

Even a fight would be better than this. Then, thank God, there is one. It starts on a walk to some remote, but touristy village in the baking heat where he sweats and complains of an itchy arse crack. I complain about him complaining, although I myself have an itch in a compromising spot that I do not whine about. Then we get lost. It is his fault of course, but then he tells me it is my fault. Women, you can't trust them with a map. And you can't. We row over the map with such volatile and irreconcilable opinions that he jumps on a bus alone, and I sit in a café that is playing *No Woman No Cry*, vibrant with sorrow.

When I return to the apartment the row continues. I wallop him across the head, he thumps me in the chest and the force of it lands me on the floor, proving to the team of women in my head that all men are wankers. Well they are, aren't they? It is in that spot we finally do the deed with relief that the argument has spared us. What? It has spared us the pretence of genuine desire and it has proven that the muscle of sadomasochism can still be flexed when you simply cannot go through it any other way.

Now we are free to get on with our books, TV, drink, thoughts.

From my balcony I watch the sun go down. I spot the map, the cause of the disagreement earlier, at my feet. There are bald patches on the streets and coastlines are eroded where the print has rubbed off.

Day 6 (morning)
Michael is in his nut-huggers wrestling with a sun-lounger. The legs will not open. He flops down on it anyway. I ring my hair out onto the sole of his foot. He reaches behind him, and latches his hand around my ankle so tightly I suck in my breath with pain.

Michael!
Just give us some oil will you?
Fuck you.

I sit on him and rub the sun lotion in, dragging my nails down his back as hard as I can. Red tracks appear where the nubbles of his spine are at their highest. A barman arrives with our cocktails, winking at me as he sets them down on the little sun table.

Day 6 (evening)
Michael stays in the apartment. It is a bad dose of sunstroke, we believe. I sit at the bar which is called 'Global Village' despite the predominantly Caucasian pallor of the clientele. The barman picks up a bell beside a dish of quartered limes and rings it. Holidaymakers appear from nowhere, and make their way, Pavlovian-style, towards the bar.

"Happy Hour," he explains to me with a companionable smile, as if we are lovers already.

I watch him twirl spirits in the air: gin, tequila, vodka. His talents please him. I can tell by the efficient way he eyes it all up, this crescent-shaped bar, his world. I will not know him long enough to despise all this. When he smiles I see that his left canine tooth, through neglect or genetic misfortune, is Cornflake coloured. No tooth – or a big manky gap – would be better than this. But I will never have to live with this glitch, so it is forgiven as I order my two-for-the-price-of-one cocktails, no ice.

Day 6 (late evening)
It is over (or nearly) with Michael.

This is what I tell the barman anyway. It is the only way to remain decent if this infidelity is to happen. Unfortunately, with barmen, you have to wait till their shift is over before you can nail it.

"Nuther-one-bites-the-dust," I say, just loud enough to be heard. I will ham up the drunkenness, get some sympathy, bring him in.

"Oh come on, lady," he has the American twinge to his accent that non-English speakers pick up from TV. He could be from Sweden, Mexico or Israel, "You seemed pretty happy earlier."

This is a backfire.

"If you knew what I put up with there," and for a few seconds I am genuinely melancholic, for now it makes perfect sense to me: I am turning into a whore if I do not find the courage to get out. That is all that is stopping me from getting married to someone I might actually love, and having two children.

"He seemed okay to me."

The barman is on Michael's side? This is not what I expected, no sly glint of an ally here. My blood turns nasty.

"Walk a mile in my shoes." I make sure that that the tone is full of self-pity. My world is a mess and I don't care any more if I have crossed the line between flirting and drowning (my sorrows, that is).

"Walk a mile in *theirs*."

"Sorry?"

"Do you ever think it might be you?"

I feel a grudging admiration for whatever woman he loves.

"Listen *amigo*, stick to what you know," I say, pointing at my glass.

He twirls the bottles in the air. One of them falls with a smash to the ground. I have made him nervous. I have spoiled his little show. Good. There is a cheer from the customers. Now see him stoop to clear up the spillage. I lean over the bar to watch. He looks up at me. He is no longer smiling.

Still Day 6

Last orders. I tell the by-now-unfriendly-barman why I will not have sex with him.

"S'not because your tooth, s'because…"

"My tooth?"

"'S yellow." I smile over the salted rim of the margarita glass.

He shakes his head in disbelief. "I'm not looking for sex. Not from you anyway."

He says this under his breath, but I hear it.

"Of course you are. Don't all barmen work in these package joints for sex? It has to be the *only* perk of the job." I drain the glass. I am an arsehole and I don't care any more who knows about it.

"That's rough, lady." He pours alcohol into a metal cocktail shaker. Shakes and pushes a fresh cocktail towards me. "On the house," he tells me.

I've had four cocktails by now. Two pina coladas, two margaritas and now this, another one. A fifth is too much, but fuck it, I must sustain inebriation to justify my actions. I gulp the drink down, crunching the ice cubes on my teeth without flinching.

Day 6 (even later)

And I would like to say that he had the integrity, or that I did, but we are human after all, and I climb the stairs with an aching

154

vagina, one part of it actually stinging, *torn*, as is the way when you are not ready, or not really interested, really. That's two rips in the last two days.

The TV is still on when I walk into the apartment and judging from the romping on it, the unsavoury channel has been located at last. But he sleeps, and like most men, he sleeps like a child. There is something I cannot resist about a sleeping man and I touch his face and kiss his forehead and whisper so many sorries that I am beheaded with grief and consider the balcony, but it is only two floors up and it would do no good. Instead, I stand on it and confront the stars and the moon, really look at them, and the barman's words come back to me. *Ever think it could be you?*

There is a warm breeze, certainly no need for a cardigan, yet a shiver moves through my body and washes up in my teeth with an unexpected chatter. I pull the doors shut and go to bed finding comfort in the triangle-shaped space around Michael's bulk.

Day 6, no, Day 7

Three or four in the morning. Every muscle, every joint aches. I am aware that Michael is not beside me. Is it over then? Has he already gone? I lever myself out of the bed, fall, pick myself up and feel my way in the dark, down to the split-level floor on my hands and knees until I reach what I think is the sofa, and instead feel Michael *on* the sofa. I pat my hand gently on what must be his jaw or chin, because I can feel his stubble. Regret nags me, as if I will only ever feel this in my dreams from now on.

"Are you ok?" I say.

"Not me. You."

"What?"

"You stink."

Just when I am thinking I deserve that comment, I realise he means it, literally. The stench of my own wind smacks me in the nose. It fills the apartment. My stomach is leaden, as if I've swallowed a sack of mauled copper coins. I heave myself back to bed and lie on it, breathing carefully through my nose. The

155

mosquito net smells too much like washing powder; the perfume off it is hideous. I can hear it too. The mosquito. Is it *in* the net then? The small of my back feels like there is a plank of wood jammed in it and it is splitting in two. I pull myself from the bed. My buttocks ache. I am going to throw up. No, the other. What's it going to be?

Both.

I swap from toilet, to sink, to toilet, knickers in limbo around my knees. I go back through my mind rewinding details of every morsel that I have eaten to see what did it. My throat clicks as I remember the cocktails, the ice cubes, slightly smelly, as they were crunched up in my mouth. I had even thanked that barman. Any time, he had smiled. And it occurs to me I thanked him for the sex too, just like that. *Any time.*

Day 8
I sleep all day. On and off. Another night passes. I am like a stone in the bed.

Day 9
I feel good again and strangely not even hungry. Michael is already up. He looks shattered. I remember that he must not have slept much in the past few days. I put my hand on his arm and rub the hairs there, thinking at the same time: this is the arm I know, the arm I am used to; thank God for this arm.

"Listen," I say.

"I know," he cuts me short. "We keep avoiding it."

Day 10
We are wishing the beach goodbye before the coach picks us up for the airport and already, when I turn my head to the apartment block, I can see the cleaners on the balcony making the place ready for the next couple who will watch TV, fight, pummel each other to the brink of rape, drink and laugh too – because we enjoyed it, now that we are leaving, at least that is what we will tell ourselves when we get back home. But before we start revising it, we must have this moment of solitude in ourselves and I don't want to see any part of his face,

not even his profile in case I recognise what agonies might be inching their way towards the thin line of his mouth. So, I sit behind him with my legs stretched out in a V so I can brace him clinically.

Silence. His hand is slightly closed on a nonexistent pebble, his wrist twitches now and again. And now his hand moves sideways and rests on my shin. What is he thinking? The son he could have? The one-bed apartment he will purchase in the commuter-belt if we break up and need to sell the house? Nothing? I tilt my face downwards into the small space of air between his back, my chest, and try to feel it, *what it is* between us, if there is anything. And there is something alright, but it is muffled, sort of stagnant; something, not good, not bad, just banked and dry; something you can only imagine that might exist in the space between the pane of glass on a double glazed window.

You'd have more trouble crossing that space than the sea before us, which is a desolation already too big to contemplate. But, it is gone for now, whatever the moment of courage was the day before. Nothing has been said, yet, and if you put a spin on it, *courage* might mean the other: staying together, and there is still a chance that we can make it, yes, there is the possibility that we have made it. Again.

ON THE FIRST DAY

KEITH JARRETT

I was late for work and feeling rough. My head never feel right.
I look back at the bed sorry to leave. Me and the bed get along
fine, you understand? It hurt to go cos we had unfinish
business. But I hurry up and dress up and swallow up all the
headache tablet I find. I look up at the clock. 9.45! No way I
could reach in fifteen minutes. Them was gonna make me do
some "data entry" or something for a group that do projeck
around here. So long as I never have to work outside lifting and
shifting that do me fine. I never wanted my first day at work
to be my last. I told myself I better run quick.

I pick up the letter them from out the door bottom, roll out
of my yard, looking down at the pager to check how things go
and I forget about the yellow sign. I buckle over one of the
metal legs sticking out so in the pavement crack and cuss out
loud. *If you have any information call Crimestoppers...* Raa! My
brother still pissing me off from the grave.

I was so piss off I forget to step over the bad-luck stone. Is this
slab in the middle of the pavement there past the tree by Dawkin
House. If you step on it, something bad happen, well, so them
say. An old woman what use to live there just step on it when a
car come up on the pavement and run her down... So them say.
Derek across the road say he step on it that day when they raid
his lock-up. And Lickle Screwface, my brother, well he must
have trample all over that stone. He just about piss everyone off,
I'm surprise he didn't get kill sooner. That was my bro though,
you understand? He was something else, for true...

My belly inside pain up. I look back on the bad-luck stone and the Crimestopper sign what say *Murder*. Maybe I shouldn't have step on it, but I don't believe in them things, so is nothing still. I kept my eye fix on the street and watch my step.

You work down through the road and it bare dog-mess you have to step round cos Sheldon House across the way is a dog-lover central. Once you reach the corner and link up with the main street, you look up and you can check the weather, the traffic, the girl them in they tight-up legging bouncing along with the Safeway bag. One shopping bag is ok, any more and it baby mumma here we come, trust.

Cross over the road, pass the next street and you reach Stamford Hill. Summer time and a whole heap of people stand up in the street just checking each other. Mans are checking bare girl. And all the girl fix up them face looking down at the cellie, styling out like it just ring. No one round here yet; is too early for man to be ramping. Only one or two people I see lean out from they window cos a ambulance screech past. Nuff people live round here from all over, but the way the curtain open anytime you hear caterwauling in the street you would've think is a village life, like there ain't something happen all the time. I look at my watch. I run.

It was almost ten o'clock and the sun already beat down pon my peel head. I didn't felt like working again. I was all looking sharp in my suit, but the weather gonna kill me, serious. A Jewish bwoy walk by head to foot in a black gown scowling something rotten. I realise it not just me feel like that.

Why, Stamford Hill gridlock for real. The 243 bus was at the stop so I just bounce on like it waiting for me. Door close and the thing start moving a lickle bit. I hold on to the railing to climb up the stair cos I still feeling wrong. My belly feel like somebody dig it out. Is now I know the meaning of that song Ma sing. *I feel like a fire shut up within my bones...*

I sit on the bus and it never move. Five minutes and we never even pass the Safeway.

I decide to run the rest of the way at the next stop. I was working down in Stokey and the day start at ten so I thought, Leanie, you better off running. Three big red fire engines scream past just to remind me my headache not going nowhere and while we were pull over I felt in my pockets for the letter I pick up. I skim through them, thinking Ma can deal with most of this. Gas bill, phone bill, this bill, that bill, brown envelope, white envelope and then just when I about to fold them back into my jacket I take another look and this one say *Mr Delroy McKenzie*.

Nobody call me Delroy. When I work I tell them Peter. My friend them call me Lean Bwoy, and it ain't nothing to do with my size. When I was in school, when the teacher call my name, say wake up Delroy, my eye them was always red. Everyone guess I was blazing twenty-four seven so the name stuck. I almost forget my name too – I never know anyone call me Delroy.

The bus was vibrating, mad. I try keep my head still and say bwoy that Thunderbird drink have to throw out now. If I was gonna be on this working flex then maybe I had to hold it down with the blazing too. Only cure for what I had was an all day conversation with my bed, but I wanted that job. I needed some cash money quick time... but not some scheming scheming dollars like Lickle Screwface used to call it. I don't have a mind for that.

While sitting there, I open up the envelope and take out the letter. I was shock, for true! Them cut up a few letter from the newspaper and have it glue down on the paper. Not nothing new I thought, but I still felt a shock when I read it out. *Your Next.* School and me never get along so good, but I know right way the difference between *Your* and *You're*. Some lickle pipsqueak must have write this.

The bus brake heavily and open up its belly. Is my time to run I thought, so I left the letter on the seat and run down and off into the street. I felt like Jonah spew out of the whale. I felt seasick. Too much movement but nothing going nowhere.

Maybe I have to careful a while, I thought, cos if the letter for real and if them *Nice Crew* got a hand in it then those bwoys don't ramp again. Pow pow you gone. I not too worry though, cos I don't meddle in nobody business. Them just want to remind me to stay so, I reckon, so I don't take after Lickle Screwie, lawd rest him soul.

Lickle Screwie, where I start? That bwoy trouble right until the end, trust. The funeral was strange, though. Is not something you expeck, cos I never think before I would go bury my lickle brother. But the world and him wife love a drama, say them *sorry*, but why you sorry I think? Is you kill him? And they turn up all kind of hour just to look round and let rip. Week before, them bad mouthing, saying *Dat bwoy good for nuttin* or *Dat bwoy need a good lick* or *Dat bwoy does need the Lawd*. So by the time him dead on the street, everbody just know to call him "Dat Bwoy" and roll them eye. Suddenly, now him dead, Lickle Screwface was an angel. *Sister McKenzie,* them say to Ma, *dat bwoy was misunderstood. Dat bwoy had so much going for him, dis worl' so heevil, we is living in the last days.*

The day them bury him, Ma dress up like pussy foot, getting carry everywhere by family I never know did exist. People I never seen in my life calling me over at the wake to tell *me*, mouth full, that is *they* run out of Red Stripe. Some of the crew spray-paint a tribute to Lickle Screwie all over the walls in the street. A picture of him face with him baseball cap and a 3D R.I.P. The likeness was too good, send a chill up my spine. That bwoy never smile one day in him life, that's why him call Screwface. Seventeen years old. 1981-1998. *Lawd have mercy.*

The worse bit when Ma throw herself on the coffin at the end of service, bawling like nobody business. Uncles come squeezing her shoulder. The reverend look at him watch. He come up to her, tell her she have to get off now. There's a lot of her to get off, she ain't no marga woman. "Afi me picknie deh, reveren'," she say. "Dat my chil', you know! Is my chil' dem tek way. Lawd, why Lawd why him?" and she scream a scream you could hear from out the street. Which is where I standing. I don't do these things again. Funeral. Wedding. Christening. All of them ram up with family I never seen before and won't see till the next one, nyamming till their heart content and begging more drink.

When I get off the bus, I run along Stamford Hill a while and catch an eyeful of gold teeth bowling towards me. It was Goldie, beaming something rotten.

"Goldie," I shout. "Is where you been?"

Goldie and I go back long time. He couldn't walk a straight line if him life depend on it. He's a breddrin though and he give me joke. My man dress up in a dressing gown and tracksuit bottom walking down the street like everything sweet and good. Serious!

He look at me and the reefer him have hanging from the side of him mouth fall down pon the street. I would have kept running but the way him stand up so, jaw on the floor, make me stop.

"Jesus, Leanie! That you? Oh my God!" He laugh loud, loud. "I'm definitely crackin–"

"What you mean is that you? Who else is me? You–"

He wave his hand so I stop. He lower his voice. "You know they told me you was dead!"

"What! Who tell you-?"

"I got some mans calling me up just now saying you was dead."

"Bwoy, that Lickle Screwie. Slice him up a couple week now."

"Yeah, I was at the funeral, you chief. You mental or what?" He laugh. I push up my eyebrow a lickle bit so he mumble, "I'm sorry, bruv. Really. Hope you're doing ok, you know. That boy was just unlucky. I'm sorry he…"

I wave him off. There ain't no way he can make Screwie rise up again with a gold mouth workout. Is just how the world go.

"But listen… listen… yeah, as I was saying, yeah, they told me someone knifed *you* up this morning. No lies!"

"Wha you mean *they*?"

"I told you. Some next mans a minute ago, started talking some shit. Said you tripped up like on the street and while you was on the floor some kids jumped you… Then I see you now running toward me." He laugh again. This bwoy laugh a lot. *How the hell he know I trip up this morning?* I let that one slide.

"Well, erm, someting not right…"

I was gonna tell him bout the letter but I decide to dash again. "Look, breddrin, we mus link up again soon, ok?"

"Eh eh. Where you running off to?"

He shout out that bit cos I run off. If I never even show up right on my first day, how could I expect to last? As for my man Goldie, he must have been smoking something trong! Telling me say them call him up to say I been kill. Bwoy! Then again, I could have done with some of that. My head like thunder and lightning.

The sky go a funny red. I look up and see a bunch of clouds and it look like it gonna start pouring of rain. I didn't got no umbrella and I didn't fancy a swim again so I run even faster down the length of Stamford Hill, right up toward Stoke Newington station. I pass the synagogue and then the Safeway on the other side of the road. I pass Sharlene place. Hope she wasn't looking out the window; is long time I don't speak to her.

Every time I'm running the sweat just drop off. As long as the suit jacket stay on you can't see me dripping, I thought, but when I look down there was a big patch in the middle. I run anyway. All the car them tooting like it a make the traffic move but I must have pass three or four bus by the time I reach the station. I was running fast. Screwie never outrun me once in him life, even though he was eight year younger than me.

There's a corner shop just by the station and I know Toni who work there. I saw a man leave the shop and Toni stand up there behind the counter with a face like Monday morning come round three days in a row. She look up just as I was about to speed out of sight. When she saw my face she look like she see a duppy and she jump over the counter and run out.

"Leanie... fuck!" Her face look like she gonna sick up any moment so I decide I better stop and see what go on.

"Hello, missie, " I say. "This how you greet me now?"

Toni just look on me. "Shit! You alive?"

I never know what to say to that. "Is what you mean... *alive*?"

"You're meant to be dead. Everyone knows that!"

"Every–?" I pause. Everyone smoking this shit part from me. *Gimme some, please.*

Is then I think, but wait, who is this Everyone? This Everyone that go calling up every last person in Tottenham, Stamford Hill, and who know where? And what him go do that for? I wonder if this Everyone reach Jamaica yet. Maybe even

163

Barbados, New York, Birmingham – anywhere that know the McKenzie family. I thought, when I find this Everyone, there gonna be hell and powder house.

"Since when?" I ask her.

Toni look at her watch, shaking her head plenty. "Since they called me twenty-five minutes ago".

I walk toward her. She put a hand to my chest but I never felt it cos it go right through. I don't know who scream louder.

GAPS

___

TAMSIN COTTIS

The night before she got Maya's text from Lake Malawi, Caz ordered the new bed. It had two separate mattresses on a king size frame. Each side had its own set of controls, enabling either person to sit up, or lie flat, independently of the other. Caz had told her husband Ed that it would help her RSI-aggravated bad back. In fact, she'd chosen it because, since their daughter had been in Africa, Ed had put on so much weight, Caz found herself squeezed up against the bedside table most nights while he occupied three quarters of the available space. Plus, if she was honest, his distended stomach was not conducive to intimacy – he was lucky she wasn't planning separate rooms. Working from home, he got little exercise, and now they no longer had Maya as an excuse to bring them together at meal times, Caz was following a high protein, no-carb diet, free of the worry that she was sending bad body-image messages to Maya. Ed, meanwhile, seemed to exist on takeaways and kettle chips. The new sleeping arrangements would be just one more thing keeping them apart.

Caz was too busy at work to miss Maya but she knew Ed felt differently. Last week she'd come downstairs and found him in the study, his face lit blue by the computer, stroking the wall with his finger.

"What the hell are you doing?" she'd asked, afraid he'd finally lost his grip. She'd heard that going freelance could do that to a person.

"There's some chipped paintwork, just here," he said, pointing to a small patch of bare plaster. "It's where Maya tipped her chair back, when she was on MSN. I told her to be careful. She never sat properly. I was terrified she'd break her neck."

For a second, Caz saw Maya's image, sitting at the screen, bony knee up at her chin, flesh poking through the rip in her jeans as she hammered the keyboard – speaking in teenage tongues and wasting time with her friends.

"I keep telling you we should redecorate in here," Caz said, leaving the room quickly, pulling the door shut behind her.

Caz never believed Maya would actually go. After all, as a little girl she'd been so clingy. Once, after an especially difficult morning, when Caz had arrived at the office with the press of Maya's two-year-old fingers still stinging her neck, she'd complained to Ed, "If only I lived somewhere where mothers wrap their babies round themselves in a big cloth and go to work in the fields, or fetch water, or whatever it is they do. Apparently, those babies never cry. They've done research and everything. And it's even worse now Maya can speak. She begged me to stay with her. I mean, actually begged. "*PLeeeease Mummy!*" she said, "*Please not work today.*"

She'd caught the rise in Ed's eyebrows, "Don't look at me like that! What am I supposed to do? We *need* two salaries."

It had always been difficult to juggle work and home. Before Maya was born, Caz thought separation was only a problem for spoiled kids and weak mothers. It had been a shock to discover that leaving your baby could feel like losing an arm. And she had been startled to hear herself, a few years later, on the phone to her manager, inventing a migraine in order to go to Maya's infant nativity play.

However, once she was made a Partner, with responsibility for the U.S. client base, it got harder to lie whenever there was something on at school. One day, when they were between au pairs and Maya was sick with chicken pox, she'd offered to buy Ed cup final tickets if he would stay at home and look after her. They were on the brink of a big new contract at work, and it had been a joke – sort of. Even so, she'd felt bad when she'd seen Maya by the door, listening. Another time, her daughter showed her a picture she'd done. "This is a drawing of my mummy going to work" she'd written on it. "She has a photo of me on her desk so she can remember me."

"Gosh, Maya," Caz said, "I do look cross in your picture."

Caz had to fight them both about a second baby. Ed worried about 'lonely onlies' and Maya had told her that all she wanted for her seventh birthday was a little sister. Caz knew it was impossible. As it was, she was always exhausted. And now they'd moved to a larger house, there was no way they could afford another set of school fees. Maya might *say* she'd prefer to go to the local primary with the cleaner's children, but she'd realise what sacrifices had been made for her when she was older. Caz was sure of that, though she had to remind herself that they were doing the right thing when Maya's secondary school grades began to slip, and again when St Edward's refused to have her in the sixth form.

"We're not sure it's the right place for her," the head teacher had said, when Maya had been caught, for the third time, bunking off lessons on the recreation ground that bordered the school's hockey field.

"What were you doing there?" Caz asked Maya. "Why were you on the swings?"

"I like watching the kids with their mums," she'd said.

While they were trying to sort out a place at the local FE college, Maya planned her Africa trip in secret. Caz was amazed. She'd never mentioned wanting to go and Christmas 2000, at the luxury Gambian resort hotel, had been a disaster. Maya, aged ten, hated the heat and cried herself to sleep each night they were there.

"How could you take me away from home!" she yelled at her parents. "I need cold weather and dark teatimes or it isn't proper Christmas."

Caz knew Maya's favourite holidays had been in the cottage in St Ives, staying next door to the family with five children and playing all day on the beach. Caz had longed for luxury under a clear blue sky, not sand in the bed and pasties, but she was overruled by Ed and Maya.

Perhaps Maya's philanthropy was Ed's fault. He'd done that Kilimanjaro climb for Save The Children, back in the days he could still fit into his Rohan trek trousers. Or maybe it was just the power of the charity telethons: those films of black children with flies in their eyes, set to sad music.

Maya only told them she was going after she'd sorted it all out – booked the flights and everything. She said it had been easy. She'd borrowed one of Caz's credit cards and by the time the statement came through, there was no changing her mind. If she'd told her she wanted to travel, Caz would have fixed for her to go with a company that would fly her round the world for six months and then – if she *insisted* on doing something useful – she would arrange for her to have a couple of weeks painting some third world nursery, or clearing a bit of rainforest, before flying home. Caz's boss had a photo of his gap-year son as his screensaver, scuba diving off the Great Barrier Reef. Caz was sure the boy had done a bit of football coaching with Filipino street children as well.

But Maya chose to go as a volunteer for a charity, to work full-time in a school, attached to a sugar plantation, a four hour road trip from Dar es Salaam. (or 'Dar', as Maya called it, as if she was already a local).

It took a whole week to pack her rucksack – cramming in notebooks, toiletries and toys to give away when she got there. There was hardly room for her own clothes – not that she cared, of course. Maya had such beautiful clothes when she was a baby. But as soon as she could dress herself, she took to wearing jogging pants and boys t-shirts and refused to even look at the Mini Boden catalogue. Once, the au pair took her to a jumble sale in the church hall, and Maya had come home beaming, wearing a ghastly acrylic sweatshirt with Disney's 'Pocahontas' on the front. After one terrible day when the au pair let her wear it to nursery for the school photo, Caz was forced to put it into the bag for Oxfam.

Maya's adolescence had been spent in smelly Converse trainers which she refused to upgrade, even when the soles were dropping off; overlong jeans, and skinny vest tops or oversized hoodies. For her 16th birthday Caz paid for her have a session with a Top Shop personal stylist, but Maya let the cleaner's daughter go in her place. "It's not like I'm even interested in all that stuff, Mum. And it was fun watching Chantelle choose what she wanted."

On the day she left, Caz, Ed and Maya had sat in Terminal 4 Starbucks, staring at the information screens, not speaking. When the flight came up, Ed gave Maya a hug and Caz watched as they briefly touched foreheads. She moved to kiss her daughter.

"Don't stress, Mum. Honestly, I'll be fine from here." Maya said, slipping her daysack over one shoulder and taking a few steps backwards, away from Caz.

"But how will we know you're safe!" Caz had been surprised by the sudden panic she felt.

"I'll call. Everyone has mobiles in Africa. Don't you know *anything.*"

Then she'd gone through passport control without turning round.

Maya's first email was full of indignation at what she found at the plantation. "It's not like they're starving or anything, but a lot of the children have no shoes. And no lunch. And the power goes off for two hours every day because there's not been enough rain for the hydroelectricity stations. *Pleeease* Mum, get rid of the fucking Land Cruiser."

Caz tried to imagine not being able to have a hot shower whenever you wanted one, and spent £150 in 'Snow and Rock' on expedition accessories for Maya, and some more sterile needles. She asked her secretary to courier them to Tanzania immediately. She Googled the South African company that owned the plantation and felt better – they seemed solid enough. It couldn't be *that* bad.

Maya's downloaded digital photos showed a classroom with rows of wooden benches for at least fifty children.

"And these are the lucky ones!!!" she'd written. "Please send pencils. And pictures of David Beckham. Also we need kiddie scissors and some of those Early Learning Centre, '*Things to Make and Do*' books. My old ones are probably still somewhere in the house. They'll be in brilliant condition – it's not like we ever did anything out of them."

Caz studied the faces of the African children. In one shot, three grinning boys leaned into the camera, crowding the frame. In another, Maya stood in the middle of a group of girls – perhaps seven or eight years old. One had a baby balanced on her narrow child-hips. There was no escaping how happy they all looked. Especially Maya.

After four months away, Maya emailed to say she was going travelling. She had some time off from the school and she and a friend were going to explore. She'd be in touch as soon as she was fixed up with a Zambian mobile.

When her next text came through, Caz was in the lift at work, heading for a tricky meeting with the Directors. She frowned into the lift mirror and applied more concealer to the shadows under her eyes. She wondered what the African sun was doing to Maya's complexion. Annoyingly, she'd refused to find room in her rucksack for the 'Cowshed' moisturiser that Caz had bought her.

The night before, having ordered the bed online, and copied Ed into her email correspondence with the Swedish manufacturer, Caz had stayed up until 2 am, preparing her notes. She finessed the case for an increase in her Departmental budget. The meeting was her chance to show how well the client list was growing and to make them realise that an enhanced package was only fair, whatever the Financial Controller might say. She knew Ed was awake late too, in his den on his laptop, but he didn't get back to her about the bed. Probably too busy with his no-hope novel, she thought. Or secretly talking to Maya.

She emailed him again, *"Assume ok with new bed. Off early tomorrow and back late. Don't need dinner"*. She hit the 'Send' key. Hard. It wasn't like *his* income was ever going to stretch to a Docklands buy-to-let.

Maya's text said, "Pls call asap," but before Caz could respond, the lift door opened and the Financial Controller stepped in. It would have to wait until after the meeting. Caz twitched her lips into a smile, and they headed for the Boardroom together.

When she called Maya back, two hours later, Caz was excited. She'd been impressive – even if she said so herself. Now she had the Board's agreement, she could put her plans in motion. Maybe she'd start looking at investment properties straight away. She wanted to tell someone all about it, but Maya's voice was faint.

"Mum, just to let you know, I'm in a clinic and I've got malaria."

At first, Caz didn't understand. It wasn't possible. Hadn't she taken her tablets? What about the all-singing, all-dancing mosquito net from Snow and Rock?

Maya's friend came on the line to explain they were on an island on Lake Malawi, seven hours by boat from the mainland. There was no hospital and no doctor, but a nurse had put Maya on a drip and a priest had come to say some prayers.

"Leave it with me," Caz said, enunciating clearly. She felt that panic again – like at the airport. "Don't worry. I'll sort everything out". She rushed down to her office and asked her secretary to cancel all appointments till lunchtime. A quick internet search told her that nothing gave complete protection against malaria. Actually, she'd had no idea that it was such a killer. She found the island on Google Earth easily enough but realised that it would take a minimum of two days to get there.

Next, Caz got through to someone high up at the insurance company, and began talking firmly about air lifts and hospitals in Johannesburg. They said they needed to deal with Maya direct. She was 18 and the policy was in her name. Caz passed on Maya's mobile number and texted her daughter again to tell her to *demand* to be flown off the island.

A few minutes later, on a breaking up line, Maya ignored Caz's question about clean needles. She told her mother that she didn't want to leave.

"I'm going to wait my place in the queue to see the doctor. There are lots of children here, all much iller than me. Didn't you know, Mum, *everyone* gets malaria? I'm going to try and get hold of some medication and then I'll get better. Or I won't. There's nothing you can do. I was only calling to say there is nothing you can do."

The phone went silent. Caz rang back immediately but couldn't get through. She headed for the street – reception would be better outside. She jabbed her finger repeatedly on the 'Call lift' button but it wouldn't come. She raced down the back stairs, losing her footing at one point, in her stupid high heels. She took off her shoes and hurried to the exit. Two people were standing in front of the revolving doors, talking. She barged between them and ran out onto the pavement. Shoes back on and frantic now, Caz tried to call Maya again, but it went straight to a female African voice, telling her the number was unobtainable. She ran across the road, dodging traffic. A cyclist squealed to a stop, almost head-butting her over the handlebars. "Fucking mad bitch!" he shouted before swerving away into the London traffic.

She hailed a cab and perched on the edge of the seat, too jittery to manage the belt buckle. "Here's fine," she said as they went across Oxford Circus. Caz jumped out and pushed a fiver through the window at the driver. Once inside the main doors to John Lewis she began ducking and weaving her way through cosmetics towards the escalators. She barely recognised the woman with the wild eyes reflected in the gleaming mirrors.

On the fourth floor she moved quickly through toys and prams. She paused in Girls Fashion: those dresses were like the ones the African children in the photos wore – before the colours faded and the smocking ripped. A shop assistant approached her, polite but not unctuous. "Can I help you, madam?"

"I'm fine thanks," Caz said, and pushed on into nursery furniture. She stopped beside a child's bed. It was made of cream-coloured wood, with three small hearts, cut out of the headboard. Maya's first proper bed had been exactly that colour. Caz sat down heavily, cushioned by the blue gingham duvet. Her chest hurt from running and her twisted ankle began to throb. Suddenly, all she wanted was to curl up and go to sleep, but she saw the assistant coming towards her again. She noted the concern on his face. "Really," she said, forcing a small smile, "I'm ok."

Slowly, she smoothed out the creases in her skirt, and felt

her breath return. Maya was ill and nothing else mattered. Caz stood up and turned to straighten the duvet. Then, cradling her iPhone in both hands, she decided to call home. It was time to talk to Ed.

TEAMWORK RESPONSE ACTION PERFORMANCE

JULIA H KING

16:09. Emma takes a payment from Mrs Uprichard. This month Mrs Uprichard has spent £7,034.56 on her credit card and is, as always, paying her balance in full. Typing the strings of numbers into her computer Emma notices a dark, viscous liquid seeping from behind her screen. She pulls the screen, grey and bulky as an aircraft hanger, towards her, and finds behind it a half-eaten Mexican Chicken sandwich in its plastic container, a balled-up crisp packet and an overturned plastic cup of hot chocolate from the vending machine. Her shoulders sag: Alex.

Alex works the early day shift at WorldConsume, an international credit card company for people who don't need credit. WorldConsume deals only with individuals whose assets exceed £1.5 million, offering exceptional levels of customer service, and the emotional labour of its staff, around the clock.

Although he has worked for the company for only six weeks – some two years less than Emma – Alex has decided that Emma's desk is his. Every day he arranges files, folders, piles of paper on the desk, pins up flowcharts and lists of phone numbers on the grey nylon panelling forming the cubicle where Emma sits. Every day Emma removes them. Emma pins up her own lists and charts but comes in the next day to find them shoved in a pile under the desk, sometimes adorned with a large, dusty trainer print. Appeals to Jim, Emma's manager, have proven fruitless. The dispute with Alex is, in fact, 'hot-desking'; ironically, since the desk is located beneath an air conditioning outlet which blasts icy air onto the back right hand side of Emma's neck for the entire duration of her four pm to midnight shift.

As she cleans her desk with a deodorant wipe, Emma asks Mrs Uprichard if there is anything else she can do, and Mrs Uprichard begins to complain. She complains about WorldConsume's decision to use an Indian call centre. She complains about the eight minutes spent on hold to get through to the Indian call centre. She complains about the fifteen minutes she waited to get through to Emma in the UK call centre after demanding to be transferred. Emma wonders whether Mrs Uprichard is the petty racist she sounds, or simply someone who's no good with accents.

"I mean, I know it isn't politically correct to say this..."

She listens, irritated, while scrolling through Mrs Uprichard's last statement. Sainsbury's, The National Trust, Saga Holidays. Boring.

She finishes the call with Mrs Uprichard and the next customer comes through.

17:04 Piera, from across the corridor, is eating an anaemic chicken and sweetcorn salad from the canteen. She is visiting Chloe, a member of Emma's team and Piera's best friend at work.

"– Titanium Mesh Bra," Chloe is telling Piera, "It's amazing. It's this titanium mesh, in these cup shapes, and it goes under your boobs, so it holds them up and you never have to wear a bra again!" She is filling in a form to close the account of a deceased customer, Mrs Pook.

"What, under your skin?" Piera rakes her salad with a small plastic fork. "How's it joined on?"

"It's bolted onto your ribcage."

"That's gross." Piera glances at the 'deceased' form Chloe is filling in. 'Mrs *Pook?*'

Piera and Chloe are in their early twenties; ten years younger than Emma. They are peacock-hued, lustrous and energetic. They have the same preternaturally shiny hair; they wear the same clothes, all puffs and swags and gathers like the garb of medieval courtiers. They accessorise. They have the same satin complexions and lithe, caramel bodies. You could cut their heads off, thinks Emma, and swap them round, and you'd never know.

"I think it's great," says Chloe. "I want it done when I'm older. Twenty-eight, maybe."

18:35. Kevin is on the line from India announcing the next customer.

"Hi Kevin, how's it going?"

Kevin's real name is Mohinder. "I'm very well. Very busy – we're 40 per cent down with staff," he replies.

He displays, Emma thinks, remarkably little irritation about this appalling state of affairs. "They opened a new call centre, offering more money, so they went. They don't have the same contracts as the UK staff. Have you got Mr Fraser's details coming through?"

An expat from Aberdeen now living in Houston, Texas, Alistair Fraser has an annual income of £93,000 and assets of £2.4M. He has been three days late paying his bill, thus incurring interest and a late payment charge. He speaks in a calm, transatlantic drawl with a hint of steel.

"You will credit the charges back to my account," he says softly. "If I see any interest on my account, Emma, even one penny, I will instruct my lawyers to contact your company, and you will be held personally responsible, Emma. Is that clear?"

Emma rolls her eyes. *Grow up.*

"I'm more than happy to apply a credit to your account today to cover the charge –"

"I don't care whether you're happy or not. It's your job, and you'll do it."

Fraser hangs up.

Emma applies the credit. She has spoken to nineteen people in two and a half hours. Her mouth is ash-dry, though she takes frequent sips of water to improve concentration and prevent fatigue. The low static hum of the building penetrates her skull.

19:15. Emma logs out and walks slowly up the corridor for her monthly review with Jim. She opens the stiff sliding glass door of Jim's office and drags it closed behind her.

Jim's natural colouring brings to mind a powdered eighteenth century dandy. Emma derives a perverse enjoyment from staring intensely into his tiny eyes, thickly fringed with black eyelashes as though mascara'd. She enjoys feeling mildly disgusted by his moist, pink lips and rosy cheeks. Jim's smile vanishes as he leans forward.

Emma has a hangnail on her right thumb. She picks at it with her index finger and looks at him as though she cares.

Jim begins to list the many ways in which she has fallen short of the standards expected of her. She has been late three times that week, three minutes late back from a break, and has spent too much time offline – getting coffee, going to the toilet.

Emma sighs and pulls at the hangnail with her teeth. It stings as it tears into her skin. She reads a flip chart to the right of Jim's head, ratty fading letters in green marker pen: *There are no menial jobs, only menial workers.*

She nods. She stops listening.

Low status stings her every hour. *I work in a call centre.* Sometimes, at parties or family weddings, she pretends she works for Rob, her boyfriend of three years who has his own, erratic, business as a web designer. Rob, and the one bedroom flat she shares with him, are the only achievements of her thirty-one years alive. She has mood swings and thrush because she eats too much sugary crap from the vending machine. She drinks too much coffee. She drinks too much.

Emma's best friend at work is Kirsty, who is studying nutritional therapy. In three months time she is going to Australia, where she has organised a sponsor, a job and a large, friendly boyfriend called Mark. Kirsty sits assembling open sandwiches from an array of organic foodstuffs spread out across her desk. She smears almond butter onto stone-ground bread; she slices beetroot and carrot with a pen knife. Kirsty is thirty-four. She has lived on a travellers' site, lived in a tree village – done the techno-crusty protester circuit. A couple of years ago she hit a wall of age, drugs and psoriasis. Someone died. She got fed up of burying her shit with a trowel.

20:10. Emma begins logging back into her systems. She has fourteen passwords, changed every thirty days. She clicks angrily on a window which won't close.

"This place, it's like the fucking Mir space station." Emma plugs in her headset and jabs AVAILABLE. Kirsty holds up her index finger – one moment please – and presses SOUND to reconnect her to her customer.

"Yes, I appreciate that Mr Baker, but all I can advise is that you ask your father to call us to authorise the increase."

Kirsty's voice is warm; big-sisterly. Emma can see her disarming a policeman at a demo with her rosy cheeks and no-nonsense charm. "That is, I'm afraid, the only way we would be able to action an increase on your spending limit at this time." She presses SILENT again and turns to Emma. "This kiddie's visiting his mate in Los Angeles and he wants to put a deposit on a Porsche but he's maxed out on his dad's account. I've been talking to him for... thirteen minutes and he still doesn't get it."

She stirs a spoonful of powdered blue-green algae into a mug of pineapple juice. "I can hear his mate in the background going 'Tell the bitch to give it up!' He's on the verge of tears, the wee twat." She laughs. "Oh, hang on, he said fuck!" Grinning, she reopens the line and adopts a solemn tone.

"I'm sorry Mr Baker, but I'm afraid if you are going to use that sort of language I *will* have to terminate the call." She presses the button triumphantly.

20:56. Emma is looking at some celebrity websites while eating a microwaved Cornish pasty.

The websites are full of salacious gossip, embarrassing revelations and abuse. Her favourite, *Celebrity Nasty,* is leading a campaign to force a mildly homophobic Hollywood comedian to admit that he is gay. Here he is, with his heavily pregnant wife who has committed the ghastly crime of allow-ing her ankles to swell up, above the damning caption: *BLOATED AND BETRAYED!* Emma has visited this website at least twice a day for several weeks. She has neither the time nor the brain power to read anything more challenging. The tiny sips of bile break up the day.

21:04. Emma takes a call from Mr Baker, who has called back from Los Angeles insisting that she increase the credit limit on his card. She refuses.

21:47. Emma's eyes ache. The light overhead flickers in her peripheral vision. She rolls her shoulders. Her calves feel stiff and full, her buttocks amorphous and saggy. She circles her feet this way and that, crosses her legs and uncrosses them. She longs to walk. She flexes and twists her spine but the area between her shoulder blades is like rock. She detects a head-ache beginning and takes two paracetamol, washing them down with coffee from the machine. She must stop this. The coffee leaves her lips numb – they have cleaned the machine but they neglected to rinse out all the cleaning fluid.

22:12. Emma opens an email from Jim asking why she was off line for seven minutes earlier that afternoon when she was not scheduled for a break. She types a reply: "In the toilet."

She looks over at the partition, at the top of Jim's head. Another email appears.

"Could you try to use your breaks for this in future?"

She is momentarily energised. Jim's, and, by extension the company's, inappropriate interest in her visits to the lavatory (is it even legal to ask an adult employee about such things?) is a justifiable grievance, surely. She is suffused with righteous indignation.

Her teeth are clamped together. Her lower teeth forced upwards until she fears they will sink into the base of her skull.

22:51. Emma logs out of her system, disentangles herself from her headset and walks out. She walks down the central corridor to the ladies. Pseudo-artistic posters: *Go That Extra Mile.* A montage of photos from the Christmas party – Jim and some other managers laughing together. Bunches of black and silver helium-filled balloons bearing the logo for the new Titanium Points service offered to especially highly-esteemed account holders. The launch of Titanium Points has also been marked by a flurry of posters; a small flock of people with staple guns in ill-fitting Titanium Points t-shirts. A cupcake, complete with the Titanium Points logo in silver and black fondant, was placed on the desk of every employee. Mournfully Emma ate her cupcake, so sweet it made her fillings sing.

Rounding the corner at the end of the corridor she sees Michelle leaning against the wall, mobile pressed to her cheek, staring at the floor. *Teamwork Response Action Performance* says the poster behind her. "I know," Michelle says, softly. "I know." She glances up and smiles weakly as Emma walks past. Emma smiles back, with big eyes. Caring. Michelle's father died the previous month. She works the same shift as Emma, and spends all ninety minutes of her break time each day on the phone to her remaining family. Rumour has it that Jim only let her take a week off. Staff shortages.

Emma turns left, turns right and walks through the greyish-pink door of the ladies. It is silent. Someone has just been in there and it smells of cheap body spray and girl shit. Even so, the relief from the low, cold buzz of electrostatic pollution is refreshing. Rustling in her bag she finds the test: blue and white and hygienic in its metallised plastic wrapper. That thing will be hanging around a landfill site for centuries. After bobbing and weaving the end of the test in the stream of her urine, she replaces the cap, and places it on the cistern behind her. Three minutes. Tiny patterns in the grey melamine back of the door. *Please leave these facilities clean as you find them.*

She is almost certain. She senses some sort of change in her body – so subtle she couldn't describe it, some change of frequency. When the three minutes are up, she reaches back, grabs the test and holds it, inches from her face. There is a strong blue line and a strong blue cross. Pregnant. The vertical line of the cross is the line that means Pregnant.

It worked. She feels animalistic. Brutal. What will Rob say?

What will she say to him? Will she be able to convince him that this was an accident, and not her unilateral plan to give meaning to her life? She has sacrificed his freedom for her own. She stares, as though the cross will evaporate before her eyes and she will be left with the horizontal line that means Not Pregnant. It is still there. Her hands feel cold. The clock on her phone says 11.08. Fifty-two minutes left.

00:06. Emma walks home, past the surging, drunken crowds; sequined girls swaying on high heels; swearing boys. Rob is out. He has left the heating on but the flat is cold. She leaves the wine in the fridge, and goes to bed and lies very still.

KONICEK

VIVIAN HASSAN-LAMBERT

Katya Tarjan leaned over the rail of the ship. Her wool coat, once so large, now strained at the chest. She loved the feeling of the ocean spray against her face and the salt air filling her nostrils.

There were only a few things Katya could remember about her father. She had played them in her mind so many times that she was no longer sure what was real and what was imagined. She remembered his black eyes, black like her sister's, and black hair, and a gold ring, long legs and bony knees. She remembered standing between his knees and he jolting her back and forth making her laugh. He called her Konicek, his little rocking horse. Even in the letter he wrote pleading with them to come to New York he'd called her Konicek. He sang them Slovak songs in the evenings and his voice was sad and mysterious and his wool clothes smelled of tobacco. It had been seven years since she had seen him – a lifetime for her. So much had happened to Katya, her mother and her sister.

The boat was a single stack with three decks. On their first day Katya had explored as much of it as she could, running through a maze of passageways and up mini flights of stairs. On their second day the Captain told her stories of how the ship had been used to take thousands of emigrants towards a place called M-I-N-N-E-S-O-T-A, and how it had been a mercy ship during the war. Now it was owned by the Swedes. It had beautiful polished woodwork and mirrors in the dining room and bar and it was filled with passengers from all over Europe.

The deck was empty now save for a few chairs nailed to the floor and a shuffleboard puck which slid back and forth as the ship moved. Katya felt tired: her mother had been sick all night and her sister had tossed and turned with every swell. A large wave hit the prow and a spray of water leapt across the deck.

"Hey, Katya," Jorgen called. "Watch you don't fall off." He was the midshipman who snuck them little packets of meat.

"Don't you worry, I know what I am doing."

She waved as he climbed a line of narrow, painted steps and disappeared over the deck. Her feet were sore from the new shoes. They were a size too big but she was lucky to have them: thick soles and laces. A mist of sea foam bounced up, dampening her cheek. She'd become an expert at walking the deck, uphill against the swell and downhill against the sway, first one foot then the other, like Frankenstein's monster who she'd seen at the movie house in Gothenburg.

★

"Von, two, buckle my ssshooo. Szreee, four, shut zee door."

Anna's oldest daughter Lottie sat on the bed studying her text. Her thick black braids brushed the pages of the book Captain Sorensen had lent them. He'd said it was a nursery rhyme everyone in America knew. He was a tall athletic man with a neatly trimmed beard. Anna enjoyed his obvious attention: it filled the empty spaces inside her which seemed to magnify as they got further from Europe. She had made so many decisions in order to survive, now it seemed her mind was falling apart, she had to concentrate on little things, on appearances and social graces.

She studied the blue silk dress which hung on a satin hanger on the back of the cabin door. It had torn so many times, she'd had to cut and re-stitch it.

As the boat swayed her stomach cramped like a fist. It had been an awful night. She'd been sick three times and she'd felt it would never end, but morning had come and the sea had calmed and some of her old energy was returning. Yesterday, after lunch, they had received the Captain's invitation to dine the next day. It made her stupidly tearful to think of it – sitting at table with linen, silver and crystal.

She looked across at Lottie. Her face was filling out now, the dark circles had gone from beneath her eyes and there was a shine to her hair. The last few months of separation had been awful and what lay ahead, Anna did not know, but they would do it, the three of them. They had come this far, they would start over, a new life in a new place. With Him.

It had been seven years since her husband had gone ahead to London, then New York. She could hardly remember his face. It had been arranged that she and the girls would follow at the end of Lottie's school term, but by the time they were packed and ready to go, it was too late: the borders had closed. For a few months there had been letters between them. She tried to cover her panic, giving him only small bits of information: a separate school had been set up for Jewish children; her sister had secured a job in Orava and her father was helping at a nearby hospital. His letters had filled her first with hope, then with blackening despair. He'd found a job on Dorset Street and rooms off the Euston Road. He was making enquiries, trying to find a way to get them out. Ten months later no mail could get through and she'd gone into the first round of hiding.

If there had been a way after the war she would have stayed in that little flat off Hviezdoslavove Square. She would have built a new life for herself there and not taken the ship to New York, but the landlord's children had returned from Prague, they needed the room, she had no money, no work.

Whatever lay ahead she needed to be with him – an anchor to the life she had known before.

The ship lurched. Anna took a breath, trying to quell the mixture of queasiness and fear.

She let her feet touch the worn carpet. "Lottie, help me up. Where is Katya?"

★

Jorgen found an excuse to go back to deck nine. The side ropes needed checking and he'd noticed a slack tarp on boat six. The girl was still there with her fiery red hair, clutching the rail as if her life depended on it. He felt sorry for her. Too young for him of course, but there was something about her, something free, fragile and wild.

The girl's mother had given Jorgen a dollar and he brought them little packets of meat from the kitchen. They devoured it as soon as their fingers touched the waxy paper: especially the older one with her dark plaits and serious eyes.

Here she was, still leaning over in her blue coat and wool scarf. Her fingers were raw from exposure and from the nails being bitten to the rim. She was like his sister: the one he hadn't seen for five years. Skinny, keeping to herself, so thoughtful. He kicked a loose puck and it slid easily across the deck. "Whoosh." She made him feel young, made him feel like he wanted to do crazy things. He stuck his arms out like an aeroplane and did bombing raids across the deck until the older Polish couple came strolling round the bend. He looked at Katya and winked. She laughed and he felt it had all been worth it, like prizing a diamond out of a stone. He kicked his heels and continued tightening the ropes, feeling her beside him like a comrade in spirit.

★

An attractive woman, the captain thought. He could imagine what horrors she had been through. He'd seen survivors in Sweden while running supplies up and down the coast, desperate, lost or separated. He'd been lucky. His ship had been lucky. Rather New York than sneaking Jews into Palestine. It was good to laugh, to forget the troubles for a night or two. Everything would be better now – the Germans had been licked and the Americans were keeping the Russians at bay.

Mrs. Tarjan was a lady, a wealthy Hebrew from Vienna or Prague. But she wasn't from there, she was from somewhere smaller and less familiar. She had pretty hair and lovely eyes and knew about theatre and music and art. She knew how to make a man feel important and that was rare. One of her

185

daughters never left her side and the other was a little strange, but what could you expect in times like these?

He craned forward and snipped a loose brown hair from his beard. He arranged the starched collar of his shirt and got his newly pressed jacket from the cabin chair, its brass buttons gleaming like little suns. He began to hum a tune. Maybe he'd even dance. They could play the 'Blue Danube' or something like Count Basie. How wonderful to know you could travel across the ocean with no fear of subs, warships or bombers.

★

The Statue of Liberty was bigger than anything the three of them had imagined. With a green sombre stare the giant lady was oblivious to the hundreds of boats which sailed by the folds of her dress. Along a rocky bank covered in thick vegetation hung huge pieces of cloth, each one as big as a house with giant red letters. W-E-L-C-O-M-E.

★

The Drotningholm sailed into port. Her single stack spewed a white cloud into a grey August sky. She had been sitting in the harbour for almost three hours while officials went on board to check papers. The apartment was ready, a camp bed in the kitchen, another in the hallway. Cakes had been bought, the Oldsmobile borrowed. How would he recognize them?

★

As the ship docked, Anna, Lottie and Katya walked down the gangplank through a torrent of tears and suitcases, onto the Port of New York, searching the crowd for his face.

THROUGH HER EYES

NINA JOSHI-RAMSEY

Ever since Roshni was a child, the name Benaras reminded her of banana juice – *ras* meaning juice. Banana-ras. Ba-na-na-ras. Benaras. She had never visited before and had never been able to take its holy status seriously, conjuring up at every mention, overripe, juiced bananas. So there she was, not only supposed to take it seriously, but burdened with an extra task. In the place where incense imbued every spare pocket of air with piety and a finger-wagging-reminder of duty to the Gods, she was going to make notes; not copious, not sparse, just the necessary.

Myth and legend had it that Benaras City had sprung suddenly, along with the River Ganges, from Lord Shiva's coiled hair. That Lord Shiva! Whatever else would one find in his hair? Lord Shiva, the God of destruction, who had that time, *created* rather than destroyed; created a river to cleanse all sins with a mere dip. Created in effect a thoroughfare. Why did people say he was the God of destruction? What was it destroying, this unquestioned cleansing of sin? At first it was only for those around the river, and those in the know, but now it was for any villager and global villager who cared to take an ox, camel, rickshaw, taxi, boat or plane, and more importantly, for whoever had the courage to dip into the murky Ganga waters.

Roshni looked at the boatman's arms, which stretched and strained in slow motion. Whispers of moonlight glinted on his dark skin. The whites of his eyes had turned red. He looked

187

down at his son snuggling at his cracked feet. The water in the river was black and strayed ahead of them, winding first this way, then that, until it disappeared, mingling with the night sky. They glided towards the centre of the city with its crumbling temples adorned with garlands of naked bulbs powered by wavering electricity.

The lilting chorus of prayers reached Roshni's ears and she made speedy notes. Then, temple bells. Danggg, danggg. Voices in the darkness hurried each other along. "Come, come, the prayers have started." Bare feet, slippers thup-thupped, slapping between hard skin and ground. Babies cried. Cymbals chimed. The boat reached the lights and the oars rested. The boatman's son woke up. The boy's father stroked his hair and the boy smiled behind a knuckle pressed to his lips. Roshni hadn't seen her own father since she was ten. Hadn't seen him, because he had died – from being unholy, according to her mother. Smoking, drinking, eating meat Roshni knew about, but she didn't know what else there had been. Her mother did. It was inevitable, her mother had insisted, through tears that appeared each time they talked about him, albeit less so with the years. Roshni's pencil moved swiftly from left to right, her head looking up, then down; scribble, scribble.

Priests, all wearing spotless white dhoti kameez, gathered for evening prayers. Each held a lantern with a hundred and eight naked flames in a pyramid shape. Roshni had burnt her mother's carpet trying to do something similar with ten naked flames during Diwali. Since then, a carefully matched rug had covered the blackened spot in their front room. The priests in front of the temples facing the river moved with grace, curving and sweeping an arm in time here, a leg balanced there, swinging their whole bodies, bowing to the chanting and drumming that reverberated through the temples, causing ripples in the water.

The flames reflected in thousands of tranced eyes as crowds of men and women followed the movements of the priests, gasping at the right moments. The chanting became louder. The tempo rose. The drums and cymbals beat harder with a brilliance and speed that Roshni's heartbeat matched. Her eyes watered. On and on the beat went, faster and faster. The priests were caught in their own exorcising whirls. All shades of pilgrims, but mostly brown, were clapping in time, dancing, some weeping, some crying out. Then, when it seemed no physical force could beat the drums any faster, red, almost bleeding hands maintained the beat for longer than Roshni could believe. Finally, just before the watchers became exhausted, with temple bells clanging in orchestration, alongside drums, priests, cymbals, and chants, all poured their hearts into the finale, drawing the evening to an end. Conch shells were blown. The priests, dripping with sweat, bowed, almost doubling over, their devotion proven for that day, the demons held off.

Pilgrims thronged to the edge of the river, holding leaf bowls, each with a flame, each seeking fulfilment of one dream or another. Lone flames were pushed out into the water – prayers sent out, each with its task. Roshni pushed out her own flame of hope. It veered left, then right, caught in the melee with everyone else's dreams. She egged it on. "Break free," she pleaded silently.

Roshni had already been for a dawn ride with the same boatman, without his son that time. On the river, she saw a Sikh in overtight shorts giving orders to swimmers in the water. "Left, left, left, right, left." Children beside him giggled and urinated with simultaneous yellow arcs into the river. Roshni wondered whether to stop them. People were going to wash their sins there, didn't they know? Women stood in the river, palms pressed together, and as the sun came up, the water twinkled with thousands of glimmers, as did the gold draped around the women's necks and wrists. Wet saris – yellow, red, green – clung to flaccid bosoms and bottoms. Roshni wondered if they all had holy thoughts as they were washing away their sins. And where *did* those sins go? Further along the river to other pilgrims also cleansing their consciences?

An old woman scraped the debris from her tongue into the water. Another blew her nose into the river. A shiny-bellied man brushed his teeth. Roshni imagined her father, also potbellied when alive, relieving himself of all sins in the river; the final stop.

At dawn, too, there was low chanting from the temples, but without the magic of the night. Washermen and women thrashed wet clothes, as if possessed. Cleanliness was indeed next to Godliness, apart from the urine making its way downstream. Further along, holy men with saffron robes gave blessings, a few reserving this act for those who paid. Children squatted with their backs to the boat and relieved their bowels in the river. Roshni couldn't help look. A dead cow floated by, brushing past her hand, making her flinch. A dead carcass, holy or not. Should she wash her hands? Where? In the water?

The boatman was looking at a newly married Nepalese couple, with paisley-shaped eyes, seeking blessings. He advised Roshni, "Come here for marriage, child. Arrange. God blessing." Roshni wondered about telling him that she was a divorcee. Shamed woman. Whore. Interchangeable terms for many. How big a gulf might appear between them if she were to tell?

Behind her on the cremation ghat, two families carried wooden stretchers with bodies wrapped in white, with red and orange flower garlands draped on top. One family squatted by the river, waiting their turn, chanting sombrely. A man stood up and kicked a dog that had started to lick the feet of the corpse. Another hound gnawed a skull at the bottom of the steps. Roshni didn't want to be vulgar and ask the boatman to stop. Instead, she craned her neck. Two bodies were already in flames, the smell like a meat barbecue with the acrid stench of burning hair. There were only men there, clad in white. At her father's funeral, there were mostly men, also clad in white, but there was no son, so she had to push the button in the crematorium. The rush of sound that followed had filled her eardrums for many years.

Later that day, Roshni walked through the innards of Benaras city and saw pigs scavenging on rubbish heaps, goats walking on spindly legs. She spotted their rectangular irises – windows to their souls. Nearby, the Durga temple had a glistening trident, with a veil tied around a prong, marking a recent goat sacrifice. She wondered if the goats around her knew. She, and maybe they, had thought Hinduism was about vegetarianism. No harm to living things.

Families overflowing with children slumbered under plastic sheets and cardboard roofs, some eating from the handouts given by visitors, or offerings from the temples, festivals-permitting. Cycle rickshaws tringed past, taking huffing-puffing passengers who were too tired to carry their own weight as well as their shopping. A sign read 'Krishna, Ganesha, Saraswati, Mahadeva? We have them all. Please come and choose your God at lezer.' Leisure spelt l-e-z-e-r, to pronounce lezer, as per the vernacular. *Choose your God at lezer.* Roshni had promised her mother an idol of Krishna, the hero of widows.

Behind her, money and silk saris, famed in Benaras, were hurriedly exchanged between desperate hands – one side desperate to sell, the other desperate to buy, a perfect market, especially with the ever-present holy discount. Squatting women with stained or missing teeth sold marigolds and sugared aniseeds as temple offerings. Roshni's skin prickled with the heat, and a coat of grime promptly attached itself to her. As she walked back to the hotel for a shower, flute tunes ribboning around corners soothed her.

When she was almost at the hotel, a widow bumped into her. Instinctively, Roshni wondered if it was a bump and snatch trick. She had been warned it wasn't safe there. But without looking up, the widow almost bent to Roshni's feet and then moved away. She betrayed no essence of life, no joy, no sadness: nothing – like the other shaven-headed widows Roshni had seen. She followed her to a Krishna ashram, where she discovered thousands of widows chanting in shifts for up to six hours at a time – for forgiveness, liberation and a cup of lentils.

Night transformed the distresses of the day. Everything that had shaken Roshni skulked into the darkness and she was left to witness the beauty and splendour of the evening worship, and the dance of fire by the men of God. It was the only way. How was she to truly enjoy the moment otherwise? Her life back home was like that. Detached from the burdens of truth. Roshni had even forgotten about the German man who had greeted her at breakfast, whom she had then seen in the night crowds: a red face in a brown sea. This was the

German whose room was across from hers in Krishna Hotel, whose door had creaked open late the night before to let in a dark boy, with matted hair, brown shirt and turned-up trousers, a tea towel hanging down one shoulder, whose door had been shut and bolted afterwards. She was upset, at least for a while, with the ubiquity of *such* men, here, there and everywhere.

The boatman's son was gesturing and making noises, which reeled in Roshi's mind back to the evening on the river. The boy's slightly upturned eyes rolled. The boatman looked at Roshni. "My boy is asking what you are doing? I say you are writing. He says please to tell him what you are writing." Silence fell between them. It wasn't only that the boy was deaf and blind. Roshni was gathering evidence but she didn't know exactly for whom or for what purpose. For her disheartened mother? Herself? Was she trying to say something about holiness? Her father? She didn't know what she would do with it yet, or what it meant. What should she read out? She didn't want the boy or his father to think she was hiding anything, or worse, that she didn't think them worthy. She reached to grasp the perfect words that would convey something to that deaf-blind boy, of what she had written, of what she had seen. The boy *lived* in the place she had written about. Would he recognise it?

Roshni looked on as the boy's father translated the words she spoke into a tapestry: the touching of cloth, cupping of ears, blowing on eyelashes, holding of hands and moving them around and around, knuckles or fingers on lips making shapes, the feeling of heartbeats, fingers tapping against their chests. Roshni plucked the words that would sing her song and as her lips moved, the boatman's entire body danced.

LESSONS IN ENGLISH

JUSTINE MANN

Yusuf sits in a corner of the library surrounded by books, each open at a diagram of a cold water system. He looks directly at the one in front of him, but his mind wanders back and forth like a restless dog. The library is comfortable and quiet; he is not hot or cold or hungry but the length of his sigh makes the girl next to him giggle. He holds his head, pressing his thumbs at the temples to make space for a cistern.

He arrived in England with life's path mapped out for him. He is to improve his English and learn plumbing. When he returns to Turkey he will make a good living installing kitchens and bathrooms for the new English immigrants. *Trust Yusuf,* he will say in English on his business card, *trained in England.* He pictures a stylish white card and sees the words embossed in silver. His nephew has drawn a cartoon picture for the logo: first a toilet which was rejected, then a man in a hat enjoying his bath.

Aside from studying, he stays in his brother Hakan's house, and works in his restaurant to repay him. Hakan's wife is mostly silent and cold but his nephew wakes him with laughter. With his precious time off he hoped to travel the country. Instead he walks to the river and sits watching the brown water sliding by; his loneliness for home like a rock on his chest.

Above the restaurant lives a woman, not so young but not yet old and her face grows more beautiful each time he sees it. There is something familiar about her, which he cannot place.

193

In the morning, before the traffic becomes too heavy, the air outside the restaurant is still fresh and sometimes the sky above the rooftops is the palest blue. There is a routine: when he hears her street door bang shut he knows she has left for work. Her hair is orange like a flame, sometimes held up in a metal claw, other times loose the way he likes it.

She looks for a bus and if there is none in sight, she comes inside for takeaway coffee, her hands paddling through her bag, looking for her purse. Sometimes she has to empty its contents onto the counter to find it: a brush, a book, a make-up bag. Fluff and crumbs follow and a spot on her forehead, between the eyes, begins to glow with sweat. He prefers to see her at the start of the day, when her face is full of hope. In the evening she looks lost, as if her day brought only disappointment.

One morning she comes in looking pale and wearing sunglasses. When Yusuf turns his back to pour, he hears the rush of her body as she slides to the floor and the glasses skid beneath the cold counter. Her body jumps in spasms as if electricity were in her veins.

"What happened?"

Hakan finds him crouched on the floor tipping bottled water onto her face. He is afraid and tugs on her arm. "What happen to you?" He shouts. The twitching stops and she snuggles onto the tiles as if she were in bed. When she comes to and tries to stand, her first words are curses. Yusuf brings her Turkish coffee, she calls it *a slap in the face.*

"When you are working you must eat, is very important."

He gives her the sticky baklava. Never before has she tasted this. She digs her fork into its middle and scoops a mouthful. He waits to see her joy at the taste of honey and pistachio; its sweetness will revive her well he thinks. She wrinkles her nose and coughs on the sludge of coffee grains at the bottom of her cup. Her cheeks grow warm and she speaks through her food: "I had a seizure."

Yusuf does not understand. Hakan shrugs and walks away, shouting over his shoulder: "Then you must go again your doctor."

She is the teacher of small children, Yusuf is the trainee plumber. They cut a deal. He will mend the tap that Rubbish Landlord has not fixed and she will teach him new words of English. She is too tall, her skin speckled with brown smudges and her crooked teeth are not so white, but it is her eyes and lips he cannot forget; they burn on his skin.

She comes inside the restaurant for the lesson every week on a Wednesday and on a Tuesday he stays up late with his homework. He is tired from studying and working and the words dance on the page. He practices aloud in the bathroom. Hakan shakes his head. "Every week you are saying same words." Yusuf wonders why he has a brother if it's only to make him angry.

"How are you, my friend? My name is Yusuf. I am a qualified plumber."

"Very good, but we don't say *my friend* here." She tells him. "In business, we say the person's name or nothing; with friends we say, *mate.*"

"How are you, mate?" He laughs and claps his hands. "I am say like man bringing the vegetable. 'WhereYouWannitMate?'"

She smiles and sips her coffee, avoiding the grains. Now she is looking at him a little differently, as if he is a puzzle. But she is the greater puzzle. "She is everyday different," he tells Hakan, but Hakan always says the same thing: "Brother, believe me, she is not for you; this one is old and sad, maybe her heart's already damaged a little. Besides, Meryem is waiting."

It is true. His sweetheart Meryem waits for him in Turkey. Since children they have been side by side, waiting for adult-hood. Their parents are happy with this match that has grown slowly. In one more year he will be qualified and they will be together again, but now she feels very far away and his skin no longer itches with her absence.

They speak once a week on a Friday and her emails are very long, telling of the family but nothing of what is in her heart. He grows tired of her questions, her wonder at such small things. She is greedy for the whole of England, a picture he cannot paint from a library or a restaurant or the side of a brown river. Besides, things are not so different, as she thinks. Burger King in Istanbul is the same as Burger King in London, fries dry as walnut twigs and tiny seeds from the bread that hide in the spaces between his teeth.

Sarah, Sarah, Sarah. The name clicks against his teeth like a cricket's trill. That night they are just two neighbours sitting in the restaurant with English books, but inside his head all he sees is his fingers caught up in her hair, her chin resting in the crook between his thumb and forefinger as he takes her face to kiss. She is very strict and sometimes he is tired. Repeat, repeat, repeat. She makes the sound, he makes the sound. To him it is the same, but not for her.

Hakan laughs. "Oh my God!" he says in Turkish; "if our father could see this English woman making a fool of us."

"Brother, shut up."

"What is he saying?" she asks, frowning.

Does she not realise that way she has of looking into his eyes is the same as a hand squeezing at his throat?

"He is jealous."

"Really?" She raises one brow doubtfully and turns to Hakan.

"Yes, he is jealous I learn quicker."

"He is jealous I *am* learn*ing* quicker."

"He is jealous *I am learning quicker.*"

"*That* I am learning quicker."

He throws up his hands. "You never say *that* first time; how I am learn it?" She looks back and he shrinks to the size of one of her school pupils.

She is wearing no wedding ring and she is staying with her food a little longer after each lesson.

Her flat is very small, just one room with a small bathroom. The bed is also a sofa. He sees her duvet peeping from behind it. To pee he must stand in the shower. To wash his hands he must first open the bathroom door.

She is wearing a white dress and when she stands in the shaft of sunlight from her window he can follow the shape of her legs. She gives him the Turkish tea he has brought and opens a bottle of wine. He takes out his tools and she watches, drinking the wine like juice then holding the glass to her cheek. He turns off the water and flushes out the rust and minerals which have collected in the pipe. When he is finished, the stream from the tap is stronger.

She is behind him. When he turns, her face is close to his and his body pulses with the need of her. It happens very quickly. They are against a wall with their mouths pressed together, then he carries her to the sofa and places his lips anywhere he finds skin. But she stops his hand before it slips beneath her dress. *Only kissing,* she says.

Afterwards, when it has grown dark and his arm is numb beneath her head, he thinks of Meryem. It is Friday. She will be waiting for her phone-call and maybe she is growing a little worried. His tools lie scattered and he wants to pick them up. When Sarah wakes she looks disappointed to see him standing there.

"I'm sorry, I must go," he says, and hates the clatter as he packs his box.

She rolls onto her stomach to watch him leave. "Don't tell your brother about us," she says. "I don't think he likes me very much."

Some nights Hakan goes home early and Yusuf stays to lock up and have a cigarette. He waits in the yard for her to call from the fire-escape steps. Once inside her room she switches off the light and moves quickly, impatiently, and her hands feel rough on his skin. *Only kissing.*

"I'm moving," she tells him one night. "Next week. Just a mile or two further out of the city."

"But you are happy here; this flat same next flat."

"This flat *is the* same *as the* next flat."

"See, you are agree with me!"

She looks away and takes a mouthful of wine. "Someone I love broke up with me here, in this very room; it's a sad place for me. I want to stop remembering."

Now Yusuf understands two things. Number one, to become completely his she must first bury a ghost and number two, what has made her seem so familiar is her sadness: inside it is a reflection of his own. He takes her hand and holds it tight in his.

"I am here now."

"You're much too young and sweet for me." She laughs and without looking at him traces a drop of wine that has slid from her mouth.

He does not tell her about Meryem. When she is happy in her new flat and they are together there, then he will tell her and they will decide what to do.

She asks for empty cardboard boxes. He saves them in the yard behind the restaurant. When rain clouds come he covers them in plastic. The pile grows. Hakan is very impatient with the *box mountain*. He kicks it whenever he passes. "How many boxes does one woman teacher need," he yells at her fire escape.

Tomorrow night is her last. Yusuf has a surprise. She must come early for a special dinner, before the restaurant opens. He slips a note through her letter box. *Come, my Darling, I want you be with me your last night.*

That morning she doesn't come for coffee. When she leaves her flat the bus is already there and he glares at the driver through the window. All day long he waits for her, until his heart is inflated like a balloon. He thinks of her when cutting cubes of meat and touching its slippery surface and when he is chopping tomatoes for salad. When he hears her return, he waits for his brother to leave.

Everything is ready, but she is not here and they must eat before Hakan returns. When he knocks at her door, there is no answer. He knocks again loudly. "Sarah!" he calls. People at the bus stop look towards him; they are bored and ready to watch this unfold: will he/won't he get an answer. The boxes for packing begin to feel heavy in his hands. They watch as he puts everything down on the pavement and knocks again. He begins to feel something is wrong and remembers the day of her fall in the restaurant and her jerking arms. He lifts the letter box, calls "Sarah!" but all he sees are carpeted steps leading to the door of her room. Music is playing very loud; no wonder she doesn't hear him!

Then he remembers the fire escape. The door is glass and he can see past the tiny kitchen into her room. He runs through the restaurant and climbs the metal steps two at a time. He finds her with her back to him wearing a towel, still busy preparing her body for this special night. She will come when she is ready. He smiles and begins to move away, but then stops. Beside her bed on the floor lies a pair of men's shoes. She turns and sees Yusuf and quickly looks towards the bathroom door where someone is coming.

Hakan finds him in the kitchen of the restaurant, scraping the food into the bin. At first Yusuf is silent, then he can contain it no longer. He throws the plates into the sink and they skid and shatter. He asks how he can do this to his own brother. Hakan pushes his hands through his hair. The tap is still running over splinters of dish. As his eyes flicker across the floor and into the corners of the restaurant he swears that everything between them was finished long ago, until he saw the boxes.

POWER TRIP

FOLUKE TAYLOR

The water swells, thick with shadows the colour of trampled grass. If this sea were a man you'd say he was edgy; a woman, you'd call her a bitch. This is African, not Caribbean sea. There's no crystal blue or coral, no telling what's underneath. Ahead of me, standing up to his hips in water, a man, sweating under a woolly hat, casts a line. Somewhere in these shadows, fish swim.

The surf rushes my bare feet. My body, weary with beer and no sleep, tenses against the cold. My toes curl in the shifting sand and water slaps at my jeans. Behind me, hotels and sunshades, framed between blue skies and golden sands, make picture postcards. What would Merva say if she could see me now? Would she say 'sorry'? 'Wish you were here'? Or, 'Mikey, I thought you didn't swim'?

It's true I don't swim much. I once saw a film about mermaids, 'water witches' my dad called them. The kind of pussy that eats you, he said. Not that I'm frightened. It's just that I don't swim much.

Two weeks after we booked the holiday, Merva decides she's not up for it.

"Mikey," she says. "It's not working."

"How you mean?"

"You don't show me no respect."

Right. Why would I argue? I reckon there are places in the world where a man can get plenty satisfaction on his own.

This place is made for satisfaction. Who wouldn't envy me,

chilling under palm trees, sipping cold beer, checking out the breasts on women selling wooden elephants for a few coins? What does Merva know about respect? Here, they call me Boss man.

"Boss man! You need pretty shirt? African mask? Fruit salad?"

I laugh but I'm not fooled. I can tell they think their sales pitch is pretty sharp. Everything is 'real African, from the Mamaland' and I'm always their 'first customer'. You can guarantee that the price is a special one for the 'soul brother' coming back to his roots. Don't they know that my roots are a five-hour plane ride away, in a city full of sharks with sharper teeth than theirs? If they knew me, they'd stop smiling. I know about hustle. I've pulled more skanks than the whole of this paradise strip. I have to tell them: "So what? You think I'm not black too?"

Now they attach themselves to Europeans with peeling skin and fat wallets. I'm happy to be left alone, but I give them a nod when they pass. In the end, you never know when you might need a little something.

Yusufa is the guy who helps with my little somethings. I met him outside the hotel when I arrived. After peeling my six-foot-four self out of that tacky tourist flight I needed a beer, some proper food and a little smoke. Yusufa sorted me out. He's slim and dark and has muscles that sit up on his bones like shiny black apples. I reckon he works out, but he says no, he just works hard. When Yusufa talks, he fiddles with his hair, twisting his baby dreads and the little goatee sprouting from his chin. I don't like people who fiddle, but he's shorter than me and does what I tell him, so I let it slide.

"Respect my brother!" Yusufa raises his fist up to touch mine. I bounce it, hard, forcing him to take a step back,

"Alright my youth." I keep my voice low.

"So what a gwaan?"

His patois jars me, but I let that slide too. I need a little something. Something sweet.

"Honey?" Yusufa looks puzzled so I trace curves in the air, and squeeze an imaginary arse to complete the picture.

His face relaxes, he nods and holds up his hand for a high five. "Honey for the boss man; no problem."

I knock his palm with the edge of my beer bottle and he waits while I finish my drink.

Town is busy. The women here don't smile like the ones on the beach. They sit behind little piles of okra and sliced cassava, pulling at their headscarves as they count money and tie the crumpled notes into cloths wrapped around their waists. These women chew with open mouths on bits of wood that stain their teeth and gums red. It's not pretty. I turn away and keep my head high above the crowd. Lost in the tangle of narrow alleyways, I step up close behind Yusufa. We pass through a covered area where I have to bend to avoid the tatters of zinc roof, sharp and rust-eaten. I cover my nose against the stink of sun-stewed fish and ignore people who call to me, or give them the palm of my free hand. Yusufa does his part, batting people away with his black apples and giving them what for in the lingo. I can't translate, but I know a good cuss when I hear it.

We're about to hit the main road and the 'other' side of town where the honey is, when an old man comes up with an armload of silver, literally, bangles and chains draped from shoulder to fingertips, and hauls them up in my face like he wants me to eat. When I try to sidestep him he steps with me, blocking the path. Yusufa wades in with some lyrics and then he and the man start to argue. I'm hot and thirsty and I don't need this right now, but this isn't my turf, so I try to be diplomatic.

"What the fuck is his problem?"

"He no want me show you good silver, " the old man says, giving Yusufa the bad eye. "Is good silver. Good for buy."

Yusufa gives him the eye back, but stays quiet and I'm left staring at a heap of shiny junk that looks like it'll be tin foil by morning. People converge from nearby alleyways, bunching up on one another to get a view. All eyes are on me.

What you need to know is that what Merva said about me, isn't true. Sure I've got respect. That's why I don't knock this old geezer out and wrap his tinsel around his windpipe. That's why I decide to do him the courtesy of glancing over his goods for a few seconds before I tell him to piss off. But while I'm pretending to look, I find myself really looking, not at his outstretched arm, but at a string of wooden beads around his neck. Sharp as a blade he clocks me clocking him, and pulls them off.

"You like?"

Before I can blink, the beads and the silver medallion hanging from them are in my hand.

"Special price for you brother."

The medallion sits, heavy as a dumbbell, in my hand. It's the size of a coaster, at least half an inch thick, engraved with a lion's head. The old man jabbers on, pushing his chest forward and pummelling it with his fist,

"No penetrate!" he shouts, loud, like he's a sideshow at the fair. "No bullet pass!" He grabs my arm and makes as if he's sawing it off with the outside edge of his hand.

"No knife cut!"

I watch as his leathery skin flaps like a chicken's neck. I could shake him off, but he's too birdlike to bother with. When I look, Yusufa's gazing into space, fiddling.

"This," says the man, smiling. "*African* protection."

His teeth are red and gritty.

You must know I don't need protection and I've got to tell you this obeah-juju-zombie crap is not my scene. I give him the money it because it's hot and I'm on a mission and when you think about it, 'Mikey-No-Bullet' is not a bad story to take back home. Besides, I'm the guy's first customer. Like I said, I got respect.

The bar where I sit and wait for Yusufa to finish his prayers is safely tucked around a corner where the sun can't reach. I sip my beer in the half-light, watching the bar girl, her boss and two skinny things who look like they should still be in school clocking me. The skinny things come over. They say they're sisters.

"Wow!" Their expressions are as exaggerated as their make-up. They run chewed fingernails over my new purchase and tell me it's nice.

I lean towards them and offer it up for a closer look.

"Ever hear a lion roar?"

Their laughter tells me they want to stick around but Yusufa appears, throws a few words in their direction and sends them packing.

"You're right," I say. "Too skinny."

Yusufa keeps a straight face.

"If you let them touch this," he says, pointing to the silver lion, "It will lose power."

"What? Like an iPod?" I allow myself a good laugh. Yusufa fiddles.

"Women and bullets," he says, "are not the same."

In the club, I feel the weight of my big man juju, as Yusufa is now calling it, resting in the crease of my chest. We take a table next to the dance floor and inhale smoke and body heat. Every so often, I pull the flannel from my back pocket to wipe sweat from my face. Yusufa keeps the drinks coming, beer for me, Coke for him until I forget that it's my money we're spending. He's right about the honey; every kind of mama you've ever dreamed about, popping and bumping their assets about the place. One girl, big tits in a tight belly top, arse bubbling in white jeans, catches my eye. As she dances, her body coils and uncoils like a charmed snake. There's something of Merva about her, the plump cheeks, a similar hang of the lip, but she's not Merva, as I find out when I beckon her with a flick of my chin and she comes straight over.

"Hey Big man," she says, waiting for the seconds to pass before Yusufa pulls a chair for her to sit down.

Her name's Aisha. Like Yusufa, she drinks coke. I think about telling Yusufa to tell the bar man to throw in a vodka on the sly 'cos truly I'm too hot for any hard-to-get shit tonight. But Aisha doesn't know about hard to get. She sits on my lap and tells me about herself; twenty-one, a student, learning English, hoping to travel to the UK, maybe go to university. The warmth of her double mango backside makes up for the dry conversation.

"That must be heavy," she says, moving closer, and I just

manage to catch her hand before she can make contact. Her eyes widen, surprised perhaps, by the strength of my grip. I surprise myself. Of course, I know there's no bling that can save me from a bullet, but let's just say that shit happens. Look at Samson and Delilah. When Aisha pulls away I relax my hold and try to make light of it, lifting the lion up for her inspection,

"Strictly look no touch," I say.

I don't catch what she says next because the music, some dated acid house, takes over. Strobe lights flicker into action and for a minute or so we are suspended in a strange movie, me holding the lion while she looks on, her face jerking through a series of bizarre expressions. It looks like she's sneering, but when the strobes shut off, her face is just as before: plump and polite.

"Look, no touch," she says, and when she laughs the white jeans vibrate against my thighs.

Yusufa reads the situation well. I give him a wad of cash to buy food and get home and he's gone. My cash flow is dwindling, but a man on a promise is generous. Aisha wants to take me home.

I should have suggested the hotel. I know that now we're here in this small room with no electricity and no running water. We could have had air con, a hot shower and room service, but it's too late now, no going back. I want to take a leak and Aisha directs me behind the house. I do my business and try not to think about what I might be pissing on. In the corner of the yard I find a crooked standpipe, tied with string to stop it collapsing onto the dirt. It gives a tiny trickle of water, which I smear over my face with one hand. I stumble on the rough ground and the lion clangs loudly against the metal pipe. I want to take it off but I start thinking about who might see it, or worse, pick it up. It's as though this lion and me have become each others' keepers. Aisha's face appears from behind the curtain at the door,

"Ssh!" she says. "You want to wake people?"

Inside, stretched out on a sponge mattress on the floor, she tells me more about her dreams; a house in New York, a Lexus, her own boutique. It's jarring, but once I'm where I want to be,

I stop listening. Inside the mango life is good. The flesh is sweet and when I squeeze, I get juice. I pump and the lion pumps too, swinging forward and back under my body.

"Ow! Be careful!" Aisha squeals and makes a grab for it but I slap her hands away and catch them tight.

"Look don't touch. Remember?"

She starts to struggle. I figure she's playing me so I hold tighter, going faster and deeper. It's hot and I need out of here. I need the hotel and a shower, I need to get this thing off of my neck. It feels like an anchor, weighing me down, slamming too hard between my chest and Aisha's head. She moans and gurgles, and then she's quiet.

People say that blood is thicker than water but blood is nothing like water, or sweat or piss. You know blood, even where there's no light to turn on and no water to wash it away. It smells like a rusty zinc roof. Aisha's not talking now. Her dreams have escaped through the hole in the side of her head. I have to get out. You must see that.

Merva should see me now, up to my waist in ocean, washing her and all those other bitches out of my skin. I baptise the lion, plunging it into the waves until the colours disappear; the flakes of silver that mask the dull iron core, the sticky red that tells its own story. If a lion commits murder who's to blame? If a woman's touch is dangerous, how much more so a woman's blood? I would ask the fisherman but he's gone, leaving me alone with the shadows.

It's true, I don't swim much, but don't think I'm scared. Understand that the time has come to take a stand, to step out and see what those big water witches are going to eat.

CONTRIBUTORS

Patsy Antoine is a writer, editor and literary consultant, and is a graduate of the Middlesex University MA Writing programme. Her short story 'Jah Goat Finds Liberty' was longlisted in the 2005 Bridport Prize and she has, for some time now, been procrastinating over the writing of her first novel.

Ginny Baily is political editor of the *Africa Research Bulletin* and co-editor of *Riptide* short story journal. Her stories and poetry have appeared in a range of journals and anthologies such as *Momaya*, *Wasafiri*, the *Warwick Review* and *Succour*. She is writing a novel set in West Africa and Devon.

Jennifer Brady is from Dublin, Ireland. She has stories published in the *Stinging Fly*, *Southword Journal*, *Incorrigibly Plural* and *These Are Our Lives*. She has written and directed a play, which was performed in Players Theatre, Trinity College in 2006. She graduated from the MPhil in Creative Writing, TCD, 2007. Her other interests include music and reading, she sings with band *Love Song Burlesque* and works in a publishing company.

Tamsin Cottis, a graduate of the Birkbeck Creative Writing Programme, works as a psychotherapist and writer. She has recently completed her first novel, *Barefoot on Sharp Stones*, and is editor and co-writer of, *Intellectual Disability, Trauma and Psychotherapy*. (*Routledge* 2008). Tamsin lives in East London with her partner and three daughters.

Amran Gaye is a Gambian writer from Banjul, currently going to school at UMBC. He is working on his first novel.

Harlem native **Michael A. Gonzales** is co-author of the groundbreaking music book *Bring the Noise: A Guide to Rap Music and Hip-Hop Culture* (Random House, 1991). He has written cover stories for *Vibe*, *Stop Smiling*, *XXL* and *Essence*.

Gonzales has penned articles and essays for *The Vibe History of HipHop* (Random House), *Vibe HipHop Divas* (Random House), *Latina*, *Best Sex Writing 2005* (Cleis Press), *Spin*, *Beats, Rhymes & Life* (Harlem Moon) and *The Village Voice*.

  In addition, his short fiction has appeared in *Trace*, *Colorlines*, *OneWorld*, *Proverbs for the People* (Kensington), *NY Press*, *Bronx Biannual* (Akashic Books), *Nat Creole.com*, *Darker Mask: Heroes from the Shadows* (Tor Books), *Brown Sugar 2: Great One Night Stands* (Simon & Schuster) and *powerHouse* magazine. Gonzales also writes for the blogs Riffs & Revolutions.com and Blackadelicpop.com. Currently he lives in Brooklyn.

Drew Gummerson's first novel *The Lodger* was a finalist in the Lambda Awards in 2002. His latest novel *Me and Mickie James* was published in July 2008. His stories have appeared in various anthologies and also been featured on BBC Radio 4. Visit him at www.drewgummerson.co.uk

Vivian Hassan-Lambert, whose family history is full of stories of migration and resettlement, was born in New York and raised in Los Angeles. Now living in London, her written work has appeared in publications and venues such as: *QWF, Jewish Chronicle, Jazz Magazine, Lillian Baylis Theatre, Brazen Radio, Baby Magazine, and Half Empty Bookcase*. She is currently finishing an MA in Writing and completing a novel set in 1960s Los Angeles

Justin Hill has been likened to a George Orwell, a boxer, and Leo Tolstoy. He attended the same school as Guy Fawkes, has written two novels and two travelogues and won – and not won – quite a few prizes. His first novel was picked by the *Washington Post* as one of the Top Novels of 2001 but was banned by the mainland Chinese government. His second novel was described as 'something to be stepped into as indulgently as a long, fragrant bath.' Inexplicably, in the winter of 1994, he was once mistaken for a Chinese Mainlander. www.justinhillauthor.com

Jonathan Holt is a London-based writer and editor who is originally from the United States. His mini-essay about T.S. Eliot, workplace creativity and death appeared in the book *Common Ground: Around Britain in 30 Writers*. 'The Experiment of Life' is his first published fiction.

Keith Jardim is from Trinidad & Tobago and Guyana. He has received several fellowships in fiction and been shortlisted for the *American Short Fiction* Award and *Glimmer Train*'s Open Fiction Contest. He has taught fiction writing, literature and English at the University of the West Indies, the University of Houston, Houston Community College, and Rice University's School of Continuing Studies. His stories have appeared in *Mississippi Review*, *Kyk-Over-Al*, *The Antigonish Review*, *Trinidad & Tobago Review*, *Atlanta Review*, *Short Story*, *Wasafiri*, *Denver Quarterly*, *Journal of Caribbean Literatures*, and *Trinidad Noir* (Akashic Books, NYC) among others. He has an MFA in Literature and Writing from Emerson College in Boston, and a PhD from the University of Houston's Literature and Creative Writing Program. He is Assistant Professor of Literature and Creative Writing at the University College of the Cayman Islands. His first book, *Under the Blue: Stories* is due in 2010; at present, he is completing a second, *The Last Migrations: Stories and a Novella*.

Keith Jarrett lives in London, where nearly all of his short fiction is set. He also writes and performs poetry in English and Spanish, winning Farrago's London Slam in 2006, and a finalist for Radio 4's Slam in 2007. A graduate of the Birkbeck Creative Writing MA, he has also been published in *The Mechanics' Institute Review 5*.

Nina Joshi, age 11, warm evening, Nairobi. Rows of tables, hundreds of scribbling kids. Won first writing competition. Age 13, military coup, bloody aftermath, left Kenya. Papergirl, cashier, waitress, chambermaid, waterpark whistleblower, programmer, etc. Age 23, Reuters graduate, career pole. Age

30+, Writing MA. Mentor Fay Weldon. Novel finally completing... Needed a little simmer...

Julia H King loved to write as a child, but in adulthood writing lost out to travel, work and relationships. In 2005 she began writing again and is currently working on a collection of short stories. After living in Spain and the US she has settled in the UK.

Sharon Maas was born in 1951 in Guyana. After leaving school she wrote feature articles for Guyana's leading newspaper; later, travel articles while hitchhiking through South America and overland to India. Her first novel was published by HarperCollins, London in 1999. She has two further published, three unpublished novels.

Justine Mann's stories have been anthologised in *Tales of the Decongested* Vol 1 (Apis Books), *Harlem River Blues* (Fish Publishing) and the UEA Creative Writing Anthology 2008. She was awarded second prize in the 2007 Fish International Short Story competition and was shortlisted for the 2008 Bridport Short Story Prize. Justine has an MA in Creative Writing from the University of East Anglia and is currently writing a novel. She lives in South East London and runs writing workshops for the Open University and the London School of Economics.

Frances Merivale has recently finished her first novel, *The Missing Track*, about a failed experimental rock musician. She has an MA in Creative Writing from Birkbeck, lives in London and works for UNICEF. 'In Transit' is her sixth published story, and in 2007 she was long-listed for the Bridport Prize. She is now working on her second novel, set on a cargo ship.

Rahul Mitra, born in Hyderabad, India, is a writer, artist, scientist and entrepreneur. He has published short stories in USA. He has completed two novels. Through his stories (and art), Rahul, tries to capture the change in the life and counterculture in India from the eighties to the present day. He lives in Hyderabad and Houston.

Catherine Selby is currently studying for her MA in Writing at Liverpool John Moores University where she completed her undergraduate degree in English with Imaginative Writing in 2002. She has had short stories published in *Pool* (Headland Publications) and in *Your Messages* (Bluechrome). She currently lives in Preston, Lancashire.

Olive Senior's books include *Shell, Over the Roofs of the World*, *Gardening in the Tropics* and *Talking of Trees* (poetry); *Summer Lightning, Arrival of the Snake-Woman* and *Discerner of Hearts* (fiction) and nonfiction works on Caribbean culture including *The Encyclopedia of Jamaican Heritage.* She is the recipient of the Commonwealth Writers Prize, among others, and lives in Toronto, Canada and Montego Bay, Jamaica

In the five years she has been writing, **Kay Sexton**'s fiction has been chosen for over twenty anthologies. Recently she was commissioned to write a short story for broadcast on national radio, has been a finalist in the *Willesden Herald* fiction contest judged by Zadie Smith, and won the Fort William Festival Contest. Her novel, *Gatekeeper*, is currently with an agent and she is working on a second novel about pornography and rivers in 1920s Hampshire.

Catherine Smith writes fiction, poetry and radio drama. In 2004 she was one of *Mslexia* magazine's 'best new women poets' and was also one of the 'Next Generation' poets (Arts Council/*Guardian*). Her first short collection, *The New Bride,* was shortlisted for the Forward First Collection Prize 2001 and her latest collection, *Lip*, was shortlisted for the Forward Best Collection Prize 2008. Her fiction has been widely published in the UK and a first short story collection, *The Biting Point,* is forthcoming from Bluechrome. She teaches creative writing for Sussex University, The Arvon Foundation and Varndean 6th Form College and is the poetry editor for *The New Writer.*

Foluke Taylor is attempting to experience multiple incarnations in one lifetime. She writes fiction and nonfiction, parents sons and daughters; teaches children and adults; works as a psychotherapist and social worker and lives, for the most part in Africa and sometimes in Europe. For sentimental and practical reasons, she has only one husband. She has published articles on the themes of education, personal and professional development and a collection of plays exploring issues around migration and asylum seeking. She writes short stories for fun and occasionally profit and is currently completing her first novel. Foluke is a director of The FoJanga Foundation for Children and Young People in The Gambia (www.fojanga.com and Facebook – friends of Fojanga). She also maintains a website www.ziondiaries.com that charts her experience, and that of her family, since moving to The Gambia in 2003.

Matt Thorne is the author of six novels, including *Eight Minutes Idle* (1999, Winner of an Encore Award) and *Cherry* (2004, longlisted for the Booker Prize). He is also the author of three children's books and has coedited two anthologies, *All Hail the New Puritans* (2000) and *Croatian Nights* (2005).

Adam Thorpe was born in Paris in 1956. He is the author of eight novels, including *Ulverton* and *Between Each Breath*, two volumes of short fiction and five poetry collections, and his work has been translated into many languages. He is currently completing a novel about Robin Hood, *Hodd*, to be published in 2009. He lives in France with his family.

Sophie Woolley is a writer and actress from London. Following a UK tour of her one person play, *When to Run*, she adapted the comedy for BBC Radio 4. Her latest play, *Fight Face,* in which she also performed, had a three week run at Hammersmith Lyric in September 2008. www.sophiewoolley.com